THE MORELLO LETTERS

THE MORELLO LETTERS

Pen pal to the Stars

MONSTER PUBLICATIONS • *London*

Second Edition
Published in Great Britain in 2009 by
Monster Publications
53a Park View Road
Ealing
London W5 2JF

2

A catalogue for this is available
from the British Library

ISBN 978-0-9563422-0-1

Printed in the UK by CPI William Clowes Beccles NR34 7TL

*To the memory of my parents,
to whom I owe everything*

25 July 2006

Dear Mr Morello

We have not been formally introduced. I and my wife Prudence and our daughter, little Peony (aged 20), are your new next door neighbours, having moved into Carbuncle Cottage just a fortnight ago. I believe you must be the gentleman constantly traipsing past the cottage and down the road to the letterbox, laden with reams of post, and usually with some farmyard animal such as a goat trailing along behind you on a string.

Hoping for gentler days we moved to Ealing after five years living on the railway estate in Dagenham. I have high blood pressure and dear Prudence developed an acute allergy to fur and feathers after a spell as receptionist at the Romford Poodle and Parrot Parlour. I am afraid that our induction into Park View Road has been far from promising. Several incidents are responsible.

On the day of our arrival one of your goats chewed all the blooms off Prudence's prize begonias, then urinated on our charming little gnome Hector, and kicked him off his mushroom.

Then, last Saturday morning, a glorious day, Prudence was in our back garden, admiring Mother Nature's seasonal bounty. The hauntingly romantic strains of that lovely Italian ballad "*O Cara Mio*" (*Oh My Heart's Delight!*) wafted across from your side of the fence. The tune was rendered by a particularly hoarse and unmelodic voice, apparently female. This was accompanied by an incongruous and ominous metallic scraping and banging noise. Suddenly a loud whooshing sound heralded the arrival of a volley of unidentifiable matter sailing over the fence and into our garden. At that precise moment Prudence, in her new spring frock, was gently sniffing the dahlias. Before any evasive action was possible, she was hit square on by an enormous volume of slurry, which splashed all over her as she let forth a scream of despair. In the most perfunctory of apologies, a well built lady in a dressing gown, curlers and huge spectacles, clutching a wire brush and dustpan, shoved her head round the end of the driveway and yelled "*I'm only mucking out the marmosets etc!*" I believe from later sightings that this apparition was in fact Mrs Morello.

1

Mr Morello, I must enquire as to precisely the arrangements in your house and garden? We had understood you ran a small bakery from the back of your home. Yet what with the random ear-splitting screeches and howls, the yodelling and the strange scratching and snuffling noises emanating from your premises, and now the unpleasant exotic dungs of which we have direct experience, we gain the distinct impression of some form of biblical Ark being assembled.

It is indeed profoundly disconcerting to be gazed at constantly over one's own back garden hedge by a camel. Or a llama.

Prudence joins me in expressing the hope that we may meet up socially to sort out any misunderstandings. Perhaps you might both join us at one of our little vegetarian prayer-and-knitting groups, so that we may get to know each other rather better.

Yours sincerely

Timothy Toogood

Timothy Toogood

PS: Prudence states she has just noticed an unusual sloth-type creature crawling across our front lawn, apparently with a small leg of something else poking out of its mouth.

Sir Michael Angus
Chairman
Boots Plc
1 Thane Road West
Beeston
Nottingham NG2 3AR

Ealing
London W5

15 August 1996

Dear Sir Michael Angus

HAIRBRUSH HORROR!

I write to you as Chairman of Boots and as a man I imagine very much on top of things, in all ways.

I recently effected purchase from your international downtown branch in Piccadilly Circus of a single black hairbrush. The remnants of my purchase are enclosed herewith.

I am not a man of a delicate disposition, but what happened in the ensuing weeks can only be described as a hairbrush horror, or possibly a cranial catastrophe.

The teeth fell out! No, not my teeth. Rather, on almost every occasion I used this implement, several of its teeth tore off. This was indisputably the effect. What however, was the cause of this nightmare situation? I can only hazard the following possibilities:-

1.   I misused the hairbrush by operating it in an overly animated way. This is impossible; I have had hair, and with it the need to use a hairbrush, for virtually my entire life. Never before has a hairbrush disintegrated upon impact with my scalp.

2.   My hair has recently assumed the consistency of a Brillo Pad. Again, not so. I am prepared to submit to medical examination on this one. My hair is silky and soft to the touch.

3.   Your hairbrush boffins have a puckish sense of humour, playing their full part in a wheeze to disarm punters of the thick end of five quid whilst leaving them after a fortnight with a worthless black stick and a load of plastic needles stuck in their head. (This is a possibility; have you noticed how in commercials on the box inventors are invariably portrayed as, a) mad, b) professors and, c) balding - cf the Teflon ad).

4.   Most of your punters are bald in the first place. This one is the most unlikely of all. Don't even attempt to run it. Whilst in your store, I saw two New Age travellers, with hair down towards their knees, the consistency of which was akin to rope with which you

3

could tether the QE2 in a force 9 gale; and a lady with a hairdo you could split a coconut on.

When on earth did anyone ever hear of a hairbrush suffering from alopecia?

You, yourself, may or may not have hair. Hence, I cannot gauge your degree of empathy.

However, to me the situation is an outrage. As a result of my dealings with your company I have suffered loss, anxiety, distress and inconvenience. I have also become - I hope temporarily - less attractive to the opposite sex who regard my unkempt state and the flecks of black plastic on and around my head as inappropriate and off putting.

This letter is not written idly. I must demand an explanation and reparation of a pecuniary nature within 7 days. Failing this, as a sign of protest, I intend to manacle myself outside your store indefinitely without cutting my hair, and to be explicit to passers-by in my condemnation of this situation.

This sad state of affairs would be as intolerable to your august forebear Jesse Boot as it would be inconvenient to me, but it is a matter of principle and I will not be deflected from the pursuit of a just cause.

Yours hirsutely

R M Morello

BOOTS
THE CHEMISTS

Customer Service and
Public Relations
Head Office
Nottingham NG2 3AA

GMR/SAW/1268597

20th August 1996

Mr R M Morello
Ealing
London
W5

Dear Mr Morello

Sir Michael Angus, our Chairman, has asked me to thank you for, and respond to, your recent letter. I was very sorry to learn of your complaint and I ask you to accept my apologies for the fact that you have had cause to write to us.

I have forwarded your letter to my colleague who is responsible for our hairbrushes and I have asked her to respond to you direct to avoid any further delay.

Thank you for writing to us.

Yours sincerely

G M Rea (Mrs)
Customer Service Manager

Boots The Chemists Ltd
Registered office
1 Thane Road West
Nottingham NG2 3AA
Registered London 928555
A subsidiary of
The Boots Company PLC

BOOTS
THE CHEMISTS

City Gate
Nottingham
NG1 5FS

Our ref: B&PCBC/RH/LB/1268597

30 August 1996

Mr R M Morello
Ealing
London
W5

Dear Mr Morello

Thank you for your recent letter, regarding Boots Hairbrush .

Please accept our sincere apologies for the fact that you have had cause to complain about this product.

In order to investigate this matter further, I have forwarded the above product to our manufacturer, and will of course contact you again with their findings.

In the meantime please find enclosed Gift Vouchers to the value of £5.00 as reimbursement for your unsatisfactory purchase, which I trust is to your satisfaction.

Thank you once again for taking the time and trouble to contact us.

Yours sincerely

Miss R Hulme
Customer Services Officer
Beauty & Personal Care Business Centre

Enc: £5.00 gift voucher

Boots The Chemists Ltd
Registered office
1 Thane Road West
Nottingham NG2 3AA
Registered London 928555
A subsidiary of
The Boots Company PLC

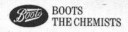

BOOTS
THE CHEMISTS

City Gate
Nottingham
NG1 5FS

Our ref: B&PCBC/RH/1268597

12 September 1996

Mr R M Morello
Ealing
London
W5

Dear Mr Morello

Further to our letter dated 30th August 1996 concerning Boots Radial Hair Brush.

I can confirm that I am now in receipt of a report from our Manufacturers who have stated that upon examination of the returned brush with the missing teeth it would appear that most of the damage would indicate that this brush has been used with a hairdryer, there is a label on the hairbrush which does have a warning stating "do not use with a hairdryer or hot water" as this will cause the hairbrush to melt and become distorted.

We are sorry that you have had cause to contact us and I trust that the gift voucher enclosed in my previous correspondence was acceptable.

Thank you for your continued co-operation throughout our investigation into your complaint.

Yours sincerely

Miss R Hulme
Customer Services Officer
Beauty & Personal Care Business Centre

Boots The Chemists Ltd
Registered office
1 Thane Road West
Nottingham NG2 3AA
Registered London 928555
A subsidiary of
The Boots Company PLC

Ealing
London, W5

2 September 1996

The General Manager
Snapple
1 Castle Yard
Richmond
SURREY
TW10 6TF

Dear Sir

I have just finished consuming a bottle of your 'Guava Mania Cocktail' (the cap is attached as proof of purchase).

Upon original purchase of the product I was reassured at the pleasant lakeside scene coupled with the encouraging slogan that the product contained 'all natural ingredients'. However, in the course of consuming this product I started to cough and gasp uncontrollably.

Having recovered, I took the opportunity to study your label more closely to find that amongst the ingredients were 'chokeberries' which appear to have been derived from 'anthocyanins'.

Would you care to hazard what in fact I have been drinking and whether these unpleasant sounding ingredients are responsible ?

Given the title of your product may I also expect imminently to experience an attack of mania?

Your sincerely

R M Morello

QUAKER
BEVERAGES UK

6 September 1996

R M Morello
Ealing, London W5

Dear R M Morello

Thank you so much for taking the time to share with us your enthusiasm for Snapple Natural Beverages, especially the flavour ending in a synonym of 'craze'. "Made from the Best Stuff on Earth" is Snapple's slogan and registered trademark and all the ingredients in Snapple are, indeed, natural in origin. Our company is dedicated to producing great-tasting, all natural drinks, with an ongoing concern for the well-being of its loyal consumers. Every one of our flavours is made from the finest all natural ingredients we can find.

We are happy to answer your question regarding chokeberries. Chokeberries are a red or purple fruit plucked from an North American rosaceous chokeberry shrub. The anthocyanins that are used to give Guava Mania Cocktail it's delicious colour are derived from (rather than the other way around) the chokeberries and from elderberries, grapes and cherries. In short, this means we are using fruit to colour our drinks rather than artificial ingredients.

We hope we this answers your questions and resolves any concerns you may have had regarding the ingredients in Guava Mania. Perhaps your coughing and gasping was due to the feather pillow you ate before you drank your Snapple?

We strive to give the consumer the best possible product we can and we take great pride when our Snapple consumers care enough to write to us to express their enjoyment or interest in our Natural Beverages.

To say thank you for your amusing letter which brightened our Friday morning, we enclose a small souvenir which we hope you will enjoy.

Thank you for writing.

Kind Regards

Cassandra La Rae
Customer Services
Quaker Beverages UK

One Castle Yard, Richmond, Surrey, TW10 6TF, England U.K.
Quaker Beverages U.K. is a Division of Quaker Trading Ltd. Registered Office: P.O. Box 24, Bridge Road, Southall, Middlesex UB2 4AG Registered in England No. 3068944

Park View Road
Ealing
London W5

24 September 2004

Ms Cassandra La Rae
Customer Services
Quaker Beverages
One Castle Yard
Richmond
Surrey TW10 6TF

Dear Ms La Rae

I apologise for the delay in replying to your letter of 6 September 1996 (copy attached, with mine to you of 2 September 1996).

In fact Mrs Morello (Rosetta) was convinced that Barry (our goat) had eaten it! There is some sense in this: Barry once ate a sock, two packets of pork scratchings, my income tax return and most of the A-D edition of the London telephone directory. This was all in one evening between the end of *Supermarket Sweep* and the beginning of *Hawaii Five-O*! He was just starting on my trousers when we caught him!

The loss of the telephone directory was a near disaster. For two years we lost contact with Ted and Doris Bostock, great friends who used to invite us to their summer holiday whist drives at Eastbourne Round Table.

In fact we've just found your letter. It was down the back of the sofa! I wanted to say what else we found down there but Mrs Morello wouldn't let me. The whole episode led to a difficult situation with our eldest Tosti (17) who has been hiding in his bedroom for the last two days, refusing to show his face.

A thousand thank yous for the souvenir *Snapple* T shirt enclosed with your last letter, 8 years ago. As you said, it's a bit small. And I have got bigger since, sideways. Any chance perhaps of an XXL? I could always eat the small one.

Do keep in touch. It's nice to receive letters. And gifts. At our new address.

Yours sincerely

RM Morello

PS: Barry passed away in 1998.

PPS: Are you still going?

Cadbury Schweppes EUROPEAN BEVERAGES

46 Clarendon Road, Watford, Hertfordshire WD17 1HR. United Kingdom.

October 21st, 2004

RM Morello
Park View Road
Ealing
London W5

Dear Mr. Morello,

A big hello from Snapple and thank you for taking the time to write to us after all these years...and Yes we are still going and Yes your letter has brought a smile to my face and of many others...

We are sad to hear about Barry although the only consolation is that he must have had a very fulfilling and enjoyable life. Surely you'll be able to retrieve old friendships now and maybe the neighbours will start talking to you again...

We are still "Made from the Best Stuff on Earth" and dedicated to producing great-tasting, all natural drinks, with an ongoing concern for the well-being of our loyal customers. Sadly our parents have also passed away in 2000 and we have now been adopted by a well known UK institution.

We were sorry to hear that your T-shirt has now become too small and am afraid that the UK marketers find the standard L size sufficient to hold. The U.S sizes are in fact much larger!! However, it is our intention to satisfy all consumer needs and therefore we hope to diversify our offer in the future.

We hope Snapple continues to quench your thirst. In the meantime, thank you for your enthusiam, regards to Mrs Morello and please keep on snappling!

Yours Sincerely

Paula.

Paula Silva
Snapple Europe

Pps. You might want to check out what Tosti is up to...when you are out and about... you know those findings behind the sofa... need some adult discussion!

 "**Cadbury Schweppes European Beverages**" is a business name of CSI Beverages EEIG, a European Economic Interest Grouping, registered in England & Wales (No. GE 000021) formed by and providing services to certain members of the Cadbury Schweppes Group of Companies. **Official address:** 46 Clarendon Road, Watford, Herts WD17 1HR. United Kingdom.

Ealing
London, W5

2 September 1996

The General Manager
The Metropole Hotel
King's Road
Brighton
East Sussex

Dear Sir

For some considerable time I have been saving my weekly mite to plan a trip to your area.

What better place to pitch camp than in your august establishment. I was thinking in terms of a three to four day slot but I might stretch it to a week if Lady Luck shines upon me in the bingo halls, and subject to the fluctuating price of vegetables - (see below).

I must freely confess that I am not, perhaps, as cosmopolitan as many of your regular guests. Indeed, before moving to London I spent many years earning a living on rural farms in a very lowly capacity. However I have had a reasonable education and, if forced, can speak freely with persons from all parts of the globe, even imitating their dialects if necessary. Toujours la politesse - even with the French and Germans !

And so to my point. I have maintained a lively interest in animals ever since my working days and to this very time keep a variety of domestic pets. Would it be acceptable to you when visiting your establishment that I bring some with me by way of company in the event that I find the local scene rather slow? I had in mind bringing my two cats (one has a slight cough) a capuchin monkey and two gerbils.

Derek (the donkey) will obviously stay at home and I will have no intention of bringing Kevin (the badger). The python does not even come into the equation (he does not have a name - any suggestions?).

I can give my personal assurance that all these animals are clean, well kempt and obedient. They will not attack other animals on the premises and I would not expect them to interfere with the guests. I will provide all their food including vegetables, and necessary 'in house' facilities.

If all this is impossible or you are fearful of some awful diplomatic fracas - no doubt you have endless elderly ladies to stay with Pekinese and Scotties - I can come alone but obviously I have to spend that extra amount of time on the telephone reassuring them as to my absence. I look forward to receiving your terms of business and subject to these you may be assured of my custom with or without my friends.

Yours sincerely

R M Morello
P.S.   Are you anywhere near the sea ? If so I would also like to bring Mack, the otter.

BRIGHTON METROPOLE
— HOTEL —

Kings Road Brighton Sussex BN1 2FU Telephone 01273 775432 Facsimile 01273 207764 Telex 877245 Guest Fax 01273 749632

Our Ref: PS/SM

6th September 1996

Mr R M Morello
Ealing
LONDON   W5

Dear Mr Morello

Thank you very much for your letter of 2nd September 1996 to the General Manager which I am responding to on his behalf.

Your letter raised a number of issues that I was unable to address as I am not knowledgeable of the requirements these animals would inevitably have. Having been advised by the RSPCA at the Head Quarters in Horsham they have informed me that the capuchin monkey is classified as a dangerous wild animal and can only be kept in licensed premises in a purpose built cage. Further, they feel it is irresponsible to move an animal such as this around the country.

With regard to Kevin the badger (I understand you were not going to bring him with you), the RSPCA feel the hotel would require a licence under a different form of legislation, and if Mac the otter is a short clawed otter a licence for this wild animal would also be required. Such licenses we do not hold and have no intention of obtaining.

We would be happy to have one dog and we would make a small charge of £7.00 per day for this animal.

Please find enclosed a brochure which gives you all the details that you have requested and if we can be of any further assistance please contact the reservations department.

Yours sincerely

PHILIP SKITCH
<u>Deputy General Manager</u>

Metropole Hotels (Holdings) Ltd a subsidiary of Lonrho Plc registered in England as company number 465603.
Registered Office: Metropole Hotel, PO Box 335, National Exhibition Centre, Birmingham B40 1PT

6 September 2004

The Director of Airspace Policy
Civil Aviation Authority
CAA House
45-59 Kingsway
London WC2B 6TE

Dear Director

I sincerely apologise for troubling you at what must be a busy time, what with everyone scrambling here there and everywhere to and from their summer holidays. I assume from your title you must be absolutely rushed off your feet making sure they all get to their flights on time without slopping their milk shakes and dropping their duty free all over the airport as they sprint down the gangways with 2 minutes left to board. And having to make sure the planes don't smash into each other as they taxi around and take off.

So I and Mrs Morello (Rosetta) regret causing any trouble but you will appreciate it is somewhat important, and pressing. It seems unimportant at first but you'll soon see what we mean.

From 25 September (a Saturday) till 14 October (a Thursday, which is inconvenient to say the least as it wipes out any chance of Wednesday afternoon bingo at the Acton Empire) Mrs Morello and I will be house-sitting for our very dear friends Constance and Phoebe at their semi in Chinchilla Drive, Hounslow (West London) as the happy couple jet off to San Francisco (in America) to renew their "wedding vows" to mark 25 years of sapphic bliss together.

So far so good. However the problem arises as Mrs Morello is constitutionally unable to be apart for any time at all from Twinkie and Crawford, our two charming, mischievous little yorkies. Yet both of them (particularly Twinkie, the more nervous of the two) cannot stand any excessive or threatening noises such as aeroplanes. Yet Chinchilla Drive is smack in the middle of the Heathrow flightpath. As if the constant ear-splitting yapping and howling that aeroplane noises set off wasn't enough, I am afraid the evidence of any such noise becomes very clear on examination of the carpet 5 minutes later. Worst of all, the naughty rascals also seem to try to mate with each other for some reason if the noise persists, yet both are little boys.

Before you ask, we can't leave either mutt at home with the children who are good for nothing, and Ken Lomax (at number 43) who always tries to help in a jam is having his verruca out on the NHS at Southend General the previous week.

So could you perhaps see fit to reroute all air traffic for the duration of our stay in Hounslow, maybe over Ealing, where the children Tosti (17), Amphora (14) and Rizzo (7) will be discouraged as the planes roar over from lying in bed all day during our absence.

This would be much appreciated. If we have to fill in a form or something please let me know. Otherwise I'll assume everything is in order and we'll not trouble to pack any babywipes for Hounslow.

Thanks again for everything -
Yours sincerely
RM Morello

Directorate of Airspace Policy

Mr RM Morello
Park View Road
Ealing
London
W5

14 October 2004

Dear Mr Morello

LONDON HEATHROW AIRPORT NOISE RESTRICTIONS

Thank you for your letter dated 6 Sep 04, asking for the restriction of aircraft movements at London Heathrow (LHR), for the duration of your stay at Chinchilla Drive, Hounslow.

Whilst this is a most unusual request, I felt it important that both Twinkie and Crawford should not suffer from any audible intrusion, particularly if they tend towards a bout of 'boyish fun' when they hear excessive noise. As you know, Yorkshire Terriers, whilst quite charming when quiet, can get quite ugly when aroused and I would not want to feel responsible for any canine unpleasantness.

My first port of call was to contact Ealing Borough Council, to see if they were happy to allow LHR traffic to overfly them, instead of Hounslow, for the period 25 Sep –14 Oct. Unfortunately, they had already an aviation embargo in place for the West London Hamster Show, so your plan to get Tosti, Amphora and Rizzo out of bed was a non-starter. I then wrote to all the airlines that utilise LHR, asking them if they were happy to accept delays to both departure and arrivals to accommodate your request. This is no mean feat as I had to write to them all, from Aardvark Airlines to Zanzibar Airways. Ironically, the only airline that objected was Alitalia, so your thoughts that we had not responded because you were Italian were unfounded. However, I only received their letter today, so sadly it looks like we missed the boat this time.

If Constance and Phoebe manage another 25 years of life together and you are asked to house sit again I am sure we can try to accommodate your request. However, I suggest you give us a bit longer to look at this. I recommend you write to this department in early 2029, when I am sure my successor, or indeed my successors, successor, or even my successors, successors successor will be happy to do his or her best.

Yours sincerely

Matthew Lee
Consultation Co-ordinator

FS 36365   INVESTOR IN PEOPLE

Park View Road
Ealing
London W5

2 January 2005

Right Honorable Charles Kennedy Esq
Leader
Liberal Democratic Party
4 Cowley Street
London SW1P 3NB

Dear Mr Kennedy

Hello and a Happy New Year to you and yours.

Here is a copy of my letter written today to the Electoral Reform Society, an outfit you may have come across in your travels etc.

What do you reckon on the idea of an "anti-votes" system? It must be a good bet for a party which no one dislikes but which is a bit vague on policies etc - eg when it hasn't been in Govt. for say a century or more and can't necessarily remember which bus stops near Downing Street etc.

Hoping to hear soon – in time to make a difference for the next Gnl. Election, which a couple of birds in the wind say is round the corner, and could be the Big One for the Libdems if they get the voting system sorted so it stacks up for them.

The only alternative me and the wife can think of for the Libs is double voting in Cornwall (a bit like Jeb Bush did v successfully in Florida the time before last). Or independence for the Western Isles and you become their PM!

With best wishes

Yours respectfully

RM Morello

PS: is it true the LibDems are full on for merger with UKIP by Easter? (if so, do watch out for the gent with the suntan).

PPS: could you oblige with a photo for Amphora (14). She thinks your "cute" but is too shy to ask.

Park View Road
Ealing
London W5

2 January 2005

The Top Person
Electoral Reform Society
6 Chancel Street
London SE1 OUU

Dear Sir or Madam

Hello! I'm Mr Morello.

In Italy we know all about elections. We like to have them about every 6 months. They're quite good fun.

A bloke I met on a bus recently doesn't think many people really like the political parties they finish up voting for, they just vote for the one they dislike less than the others. He went on about this quite a bit, from Chessington all the way to Ealing (no. 65). But he had a suit on. He made me miss my stop. I believe he also had a hat.

The wife thought about this and reckons we should only be allowed to vote against candidates. Whoever's left with least anti-votes wins! Then also the littler parties might have a chance. It's much better to let everyone have a go, like what they do in Italy innit?

Could we get this in in time for an election this year possibly?

Hoping to hear soon. Thanks a lot for all your help

Yours sincerely

RM Morello

PS: We could have prizes for runners up etc, so the Tories will still want to take part. And won't feel so bad about the result.

PPS: Our youngest Rizzo (aged 7) reckons the party leaders should go in the jungle and eat things from under leaves etc to decide the outcome. I wasn't sure whether to mention this.

cc: Charles Kennedy, Liberal Democratic Party

HOUSE OF COMMONS

LONDON SW1A 0AA

Mr R. M. Morello
Park View Road
Ealing
W5

8th February 2005

Dear Mr Morello,

Thank you very much for your very interesting suggestions regarding the possible improvements to the electoral system. Please accept my apologies for the delay in responding to said letter.

I really do appreciate you taking the time to write to me and was very interested to read your comments. It is always good to receive feedback from people like yourself who follow events in British politics with such interest.

Can I just reassure you that the Liberal Democrats will **not** be merging with UKIP by Easter. Also as requested, please find enclosed a signed picture for Amphora.

Thank you once again for the taking the time to write.

Yours sincerely

The Rt. Hon. Charles Kennedy MP
(Dictated by Mr Kennedy and sighed in his absence)

The Rt Hon Charles Kennedy MP, Leader of the Liberal Democrats

www.charleskennedy.org.uk

Park View Road
Ealing
London W5
9 September 2005

Right Honourable Charles Kennedy Esq MP
Leader – Liberal Democrat Party
House of Commons
London SW1A OAA

Dear Mr Kennedy

Please can I and the wife (Rosetta) thank you very much for your letter of 8 February, replying to ours of 2nd Jan.

In fact we only received yours last week. So it took about 9 months to travel 10 miles from SW1 to over here in Ealing. The wife is laid up at present with painful feet – and has some spare time. She worked out that your letter moved towards us after posting at 0.01mph (approx) on average , which she says is definitely faster than if you'd glued the letter to a small snail (lame) walking slowly (backwards, away from Ealing), probably.

Anyway in the meantime you did ok in the Genl. Election, so the wife thinks it was wise to ditch the UKIP merger, tho we did hear (probably nonsense) that Robert Kilroy-Silk is set on joining the Lib Dems in a front bench position.   I would get him started on something to do with the Post Office which needs attention under the attention and guidance of a strong and original leader such as yourself. But nothing to do with diplomats etc as he could go wrong there.

We had a few friends round for tea on Sunday to decipher the signature on your letter. The Top Three guesses were:

    1 S Nomibya

    2 S N O'Malley

    3

Are any of these close? We just wondered.

Yours sincerely

RM Morello

PS we never got the pic for Amphora. Is it possible you could oblige the lass?

Park View Road
Ealing
London W5

9 September 2004

The Head of Soft Furnishings
Selfridges
Oxford Street
London W1

Dear Sir or Madame

I and Mrs Morello (Rosetta) have recently relocated to London after many happy years on a modest but lovely dairy farm in Devon and are just settling into our new life here.

Mrs Morello moves badly (she has very painful feet) and is on the waiting list for a guide dog to assist her ambulations. Meanwhile all she has for such help is our goat, Enoch, who has travelled up with us from Devon.

We are presently furnishing our new home in the manner of a country cottage insofar as available fabrics and furnishings permit, and we have been strongly recommended to visit your outlet for this purpose. Would there be a particular time that would be most convenient to attend at your soft furnishings department?

Mrs Morello (who is rather large) wants especially to try out some super king size mattresses, and will feel much reassured to have the friendly (usually) face of a familiar and much loved goat to hand. Enoch won't be any trouble at all. He's a game little fellow, though rather nervous when inside unfamiliar buildings. So he may be wearing a nappy.

He'll have little interest in eating the furnishings as long as I bring a bucket of carrots. I hope I remember!

We look forward to hearing. Otherwise we'll come along probably some time later this month.

Thanking you,

Yours most sincerely

RM Morello.

SELFRIDGES&Cº

Mr R M Morello
Park View Road
Ealing
London
W5

16th September 2004

Reference: 1034076

Dear Mr Morello,

Thank you for your letter dated 9th September 2004, regarding your proposed visit to our Oxford Street store. I was pleased to hear that Selfridges has been strongly recommended to you, after your recent relocation from Devon.

We have a large soft furnishings department on our 4th floor and Janice Litchmore, Sales Manager of the area would be pleased to arrange an appointment for you to visit at a mutually convenient time. Sadly, in the interest of health and safety we would not be able to accommodate access for your goat, Enoch. Whilst we allow professionally trained Guide Dogs into the store, we feel that the interest Enoch would generate would hamper your visit.

If you would kindly call me on the Customer Relations telephone number printed below, we can further discuss your requirements in order that you and your wife may enjoy a special shopping experience at Selfridges. We have specific arrangements in place to ensure people who have mobility constraints can freely access all areas of our stores.

Thank you for taking the time to contact us and I look forward to hearing from you in the near future.

Yours sincerely,

James Roe
Selfridges Connect

Selfridges PO Box 5157 Leicester LE3 1ZW
Selfridges Retail Ltd Registration England 97117 Registered Office 400 Oxford Street London W1A 1AB

Park View Road
Ealing
London W5

10 September 2004

The Chief Druid
The Order of Bards, Druids and Ovates
PO Box 1333
Lewes
East Sussex BN7 3ZG

Your Eminence:

The wife and I have long been interested in the Druidic movement.

So we intend shortly to open a small shop in the Acton area to be named *"Druids R Us"* – *"catering for all your pagan and heathen requirements."*

The intention is for this to be a friendly little place, not at all out of keeping with the other stores in the vicinity, and with the accent very much on openness, accessibility and common sense. Dignity and discretion will be the key words.

We aim to stock a good selection of vestments, headdresses, copperware, and a wide variety of candles. There will be a separate area at the far end of the shop for backpackers and cave-dwellers.

Would you do us the honour of attending the opening of what we believe may be a unique venture in druidism. We hope the occasion will be relaxed and informal. The public will be welcome and plans are afoot to provide tea and nibbles. Head-dresses are optional.

Irene from the hair salon next door is coming, and we also expect Betty Thomas matron of nearby Sunnyviews Old Folks Home. We are hoping that the Reverend Wayne Jenkins (B.Ed.), the local vicar, will say a few words.

And so to the date. We've now missed the Feast of Lugh for this year, and we always find the winter solstice creeps up on us in no time at all – 3 weeks before Hetty Mainbrace has her Christmas Donkey Drive. We thought 30 October would be a nice date so as not to interfere with celebrations for Samhain.

It would be a great privilege if you could attend. There's easy parking at the rear of the store, or we can meet you off the train at East Acton station if you're travelling with full robes.

Yours most respectfully

RM Morello

**THE ORDER OF
BARDS OVATES
AND DRUIDS**

**CAIRDEAS
MÓR SHAOGHAL
NAN DRUIDH**

DEAR MR MORELLO,
THANK YOU FOR YOUR LETTER
ABOUT YOUR SHOP. SADLY PHILIP
IS IN NEW ZEALAND UNTIL
DECEMBER SO WILL NOT BE ABLE
TO ATTEND. GOOD LUCK WITH THE
OPENING DAY!

Yours under the Oaks,

END OF CORRESPONDENCE

Please excuse the informality of this note - it enables us to write to you more quickly
THE SECRETARY OBOD PO BOX 1333 LEWES E.SUSSEX BN7 1DX ENGLAND

23

Park View Road
Ealing
London W5

15 September 2004

The Chairman
Arsenal Football Club
Avenell Road
Highbury
London N5 1BU

Dear Sir

Last Saturday night I ate too much cheese (buffalo mozarella) after *"Match of the Day"* and had a bad dream. Then it became better and to my amazement I found myself flying into the Arsenal football ground, and it was 1893!

I was then introduced to all the team standing around the middle of the pitch in long white shorts and red tops, and almost all wearing big moustaches. The names of the players were:

> Alfred Entwhistle
> Henry Haddock
> Jesmond Tyrrell
> Ernest Shadbolt
> Arthur Seagrove (captain)
> William Westerbrook
> George Fitzpatrick
> Stanley Featherstonhaugh (pronounced Fanshaw)
> Percy Stannard
> Albert Ollerenshaw
> Walter Higginbottom
> and Robert Staunton (sub).

Several were talking in low voices, muttering about the weather. I also heard reference to Gladstone and his bloody taxes. I remember also a long wooden trestle table at the edge of the pitch by a tunnel, and a huge tea urn at one end.

The weather was very dark and gloomy. Suddenly the skies opened and a deluge began. Then I recall all the players, led by a fat elderly gentleman in a suit and with a huge white moustache (I think Sir Thomas Higginson or something), walking fast down the tunnel between two spectator stands, through a wide gate and across the road to a pub, followed by a scruffy boy leading a large horse. Then the sun came out and I woke up!

Could you let me know if your records indicate that any of this is accurate, since if so I think I should go on television.

Excuse my ignorance (I am Italian), but are you the same club as Tottenham Hotspurs?

Please mark the envelope clearly for me only. Mrs Morello (Rosetta) was indignant I should write no such letter, as otherwise she would leave me. On second thoughts please feel free to address your reply to her.

Yours sincerely
RM Morello

24

Arsenal

ARSENAL STADIUM
HIGHBURY, LONDON N5 1BU

E-MAIL: info@arsenal.co.uk

Dear Mr Morello

September 21, 2004

I read your letter with interest and can I say firstly that Match of the Day and buffalo mozzarella are a sure-fire recipe for football based dreams.

Secondly, having studied the history books, I can confirm that your line-up of moustachioed Gunners must have been playing under pseudonyms, as there were no such magnificently monikered men on the Gunners books during that season, our first in the football league as you are doubtless aware.

Perhaps your body of men would have actually performed better than the then Woolwich Arsenal team, who finished the season ninth in Division Two. In the entire history of the Club we have only finished below this mark on one occasion – tenth in 1896/87.

Many thanks for your amusing correspondence, keep up the support and regards to Mrs Morello.

Yours sincerely,

Andy Exley (Publications Manager)

PS I can confirm that we are not, and never have been, the same club as Tottenham Hotspurs.

Arsenal.com

MORELLO'S

Cakes and Fancies and allsorts

Park View Road
Ealing
London W5
24 September 2004

David Davis Esq
Chief Executive
The Football Association
16 Lancaster Gate
London W2 3LW

Dear Sir

Morello's Cakes and Fancies

I would like to apply for consideration of the above business as an "FA Partner" to be an official supplier to the Football Association. We understand you are well covered in other areas what with the likes of McDonald's, Carlsberg, Nationwide and Pepsi as your present FA Partners.

But there is surely a little gap here, and this is where we could really help as another FA Partner specially for catering things. We can supply lots of fresh, home baked cakes and fancies of all descriptions, with or without jam. We are a nice friendly business, with that sort of special personal touch in things. We use fresh ingredients most of the time, and we supply napkins for eaters when we have any around.

We can deliver onto your site at 2 or 3 hours notice around bits of London when Sammy is in. We have two small vans, a motor cycle with sidecar (for Mrs Morello) and a staff of 3 and sometimes 4, for the bigger events. We have lots of special lines. I'll come round with some samples when you're in. There are lots like:

> Fondant fancies
> Chocolate-encased Cakelets
> Crunchy whatnots
> Macaroons
> Delicate showboats
> Minty meringues etc etc

I could go on, and will do when I come round one day.

Do you like your tea on your lap or sitting at the table? We can do pretty place markers and we can also lightly dust the food with sugar. And chocolate powder if you want it.

We bring a cheery fun approach to multiple catering. We are a happy bunch and once did a job for Cricklewood Rangers FC ladies team, who liked Sammy. So please choose us.

Please consider us for this important roll. Could you let us know possibly by about Wednesday?

We can sometimes do sausage rolls occasionally, on Tuesdays. And Thursdays.

Yours sincerely

RM Morello

Patron
Her Majesty The Queen
President
HRH The Duke of York, KCVO, ADC

The Football Association
25 Soho Square London
W1D 4FA

Visit
www.TheFA.com

Reference RMM/RK/261104

26th November 2004

R M Morello
Morello's
Park View Road
Ealing
London W5

Dear Mr Morello

Thank you for your letter regarding Morello's Cakes and Fancies, which has been passed to me.

We would like to thank you for your very kind letter, applying to be an official supplier to The Football Association, however all catering is supplied by the venues we work with, of which we are under contract with.

Kind regards

Yours sincerely

Rachael Kerry
Assistant to FA Executive / International Relations

The Football Association Limited Registered Office 25 Soho Square London W1D 4FA Incorporated in London Registration Number 77797

Park View Road
Ealing
London W5

29 September 2004

Rt Hon John Prescott MP
Deputy Prime Minister
26 Whitehall
London SW1A 2WH

Dear Mr Prescott

I write respectfully but with some trepidation to make a small request. It is a little unusual perhaps but a matter to which we hope you may accede when you appreciate what motivates our letter.

Mrs Morello and I have three children, the youngest being Rizzo (7). He has been a thorn in our side for some time, coming last in most subjects at school and no good at all at sports. However the one thing that has caught his interest is animals – from every corner of that kingdom in fact. As a result and in the hope of settling him down, Mrs Morello (Rosetta) and I have bought him various pets. But he has got in the annoying habit of claiming people he sees bear a resemblance to them. At school this has become an obsession, to the extent his class teacher has set a project whereby each child has to produce a photo of a family or neighbour's pet, and also of a friend or famous person they claim the animal resembles.

We had no such thing at school. But it has quite excited little Rizzo who at long last is able to involve himself in something which he feels he can do on the same terms as his classmates. His little bull terrier Wendy (sold to us incidentally as Winston but urgently renamed!) has produced a litter of 3 pups, tough little fellows now 4 weeks old with eyes open, and with bits of fur. Rizzo saw you on television by chance and shouted out "Wedny" (he can't get the name quite right).

We would like to respectfully ask if you would object if Rizzo could name one of the little mites in your honour, we thought Prezza or perhaps just plain Johnno? We appreciate this is an unusual request but hope you will feel able to agree given the exceptional circumstances on this occasion. Rizzo has a particular mite in mind, and we could send you a photograph of it if that would assist in the decision making process? He would be thrilled if you were to agree!

Otherwise if it's not possible we can apply to someone else for help. Mrs Morello feels quite strongly that one of the other pups looks quite like Magnus Magnusson.

Thank you so much for your attention to this matter,

Yours sincerely

RM Morello

HOUSE OF COMMONS
LONDON SW1A 0AA

The Office of the
Deputy Prime Minister

6th October 2004

Dear Mr Morello

Thank you for your letter to John Prescott MP dated 29th September.

Mr Prescott is content for your son Rizzo to name one of Wendy's puppies in his
honour.

Yours sincerely

Della Georgeson
Parliamentary Office Manager to **The Rt Hon John Prescott MP**
Deputy Prime Minister

Mr R M Morello
Park View Road
Ealing
London
W5

Park View Road
Ealing
London W5

29 September 2004

Alexander Thynne
  - The Marquis of Bath
Longleat House
Warminster
Wiltshire

Dear Sir Marquis of Bath

I write respectfully but with some trepidation to make a small request. It is a little unusual perhaps but a matter to which we hope you may accede when you appreciate what motivates our letter.

Mrs Morello and I have three children, the youngest being Rizzo (7). He has been a thorn in our side for some time, coming last in most subjects at school and no good at all at sports. However the one thing that has caught his interest is animals – from every corner of that kingdom in fact. As a result and in the hope of settling him down, Mrs Morello (Rosetta) and I have bought him various little pets. But he has got in the annoying habit of claiming people he sees bear a resemblance to them. At school this has become an obsession, to the extent his class teacher has set a project whereby each child has to produce a photo of a family or neighbour's pet, and also of a friend or famous person they claim the animal resembles.

We had no such thing at school. But it has quite excited little Rizzo who at long last is able to involve himself in something which he feels he can do on the same terms as his classmates. His little gerbil Dandy (sold to us incidentally as Derek but urgently renamed!) has produced a litter of 8 babies, now 2 weeks old with eyes open, and bits of fur. Rizzo saw you on television by chance and shouted out "*gebrils*" (he can't get the name quite right).

We would like to respectfully ask if you would object if Rizzo could name one of the little mites in your honour, we thought Alex or perhaps just plain Al? We appreciate this is an unusual request but hope you will feel able to agree given the exceptional circumstances on this occasion. Rizzo has a particular mite in mind, and we could send you a photograph of it if that would assist in the decision making process? He would be thrilled if you were to agree!

Otherwise if it's not possible we can apply to someone else for help. Mrs Morello feels quite strongly that one of the other babies looks quite like Sir Cliff Richard.

Thank you so much for your attention to this small matter,

Yours sincerely

RM Morello

30

From: ALEXANDER THYNN, THE MARQUESS OF BATH, LONGLEAT HOUSE, WILTSHIRE / WESSEX, GB: BA12 7NN

Motorways: M3 Exit 8; A303 past Andover towards Exeter; Exit for Warminster. M4 Exit 17 towards Chippenham; then towards Warminster
Stations: Westbury from Paddington; Warminster from Waterloo (change at Salisbury). *website:* www.lordbath.co.uk

Dear Mr Morello

I shall be delighted if Rizzo chooses to call name one of his young gerbils by the name of Alex. I hope he behaves himself!

Sincerely

Bath

Park View Road
Ealing
London W5

20 October 2004

Alexander Thynn
 - The Marquis of Bath
Longleat House
Wiltshire
BA12 7NN

Dear Bath

I hope I may address you in this manner which I understand is proper in your circles.

Could I express my family's gratitude at your gracious consent to one of the tiny gerbil mites bearing your name Alex. We all prefer this really to "Bath", which is a bit domestic. But "Alexander" has a heroic, epic feel to it, of the sort a young gerbil starting out in life should feel he must aim to live up to, somehow.

In fact there's been quite a scrum by all sorts to get in on the action in having one of Rizzo's baby pets named after them. You name it, they're in on it: the Archbishop of Canterbury (gerbil), the Deputy Prime Minister (bull terrier pup), Cilla Black (sparrowhawk), Rod Stewart (Chinese stoat), Sir Paul Condon (ant eater) etc etc. They're all piling in! We're so glad your p.c. arrived in time.

In fact to honour this we've chosen a special furry gerb for you – it's quite a rodent which has already nipped several bigger fry and even threatens Enoch (the goat) when he approaches the cage. "Alex" has got tough sturdy legs and a colossal run rate on the tiny wheel. We're hoping he'll be mating in no time, with lots of different lady gerbs. We felt you might approve.

Mrs Morello wondered if you might be able to come to tea one afternoon to see the little chap – he would love to see you, as would Rizzo. You both love animals, though your other interests are probably rather wider. Would Sunday 21 November be convenient, say about 3pm? We could meet you off the train at Ealing Broadway (Central and District lines) unless you're coming by lion.

Yours respectfully

RM Morello

PS: don't worry about presents etc for Alex, though a stag beetle or other crunchy insect could be appreciated.

PPS: we thought Battenburg slices and macaroons might be nice.

website: **www.lordbath.co.uk**

VT/270

26th November 2004

R M Morello Esq
Park View Road
Ealing
London W5

Dear Mr Morello

Thank you for your letter of 20th October and I was delighted to hear that young Alex is thriving. I hope he has as happy a life as I have had.

Unfortunately I have to be at Longleat on Sunday 21st November and therefore unable to bring Alex a stag beetle for afternoon tea – but do please pass him a macaroon with my compliments.

Yours sincerely

Voop

The Marquess of Bath
Dictated by Lord Bath but signed in his absence

Stations: Westbury from Paddington; Warminster from Waterloo (change at Salisbury)
Motorways: M3 Exit 8; A303 past Andover towards Exeter; Exit for Warminster
M4 Exit 17 towards Chippenham; then towards Warminster

Park View Road
Ealing
London W5

4 January 2005

Ms Kate Harris
Archivist
Longleat House
Wiltshire BA12 7NN

Dear Ma'am

The Duke of Bath recently graciously consented to the use of his name (Alexander) by one of the baby gerbils owned by our youngest, Rizzo (7). Alex is very happy, and thoroughly enjoyed Christmas. He ate a nut and a couple of tangerines.

We all saw you on the BBC's *"Animal Park"* with Ben Fogle, the naturist. The wife noted that all the animals at Longleat are marrying beasts from other zoos.

During the programme she spotted a few rats with long tails running around the basement, and thought they looked lonely.

Mrs M asks if Alex could be "introduced" to one or two of the lady rats, under controlled circumstances, possibly supervised by His Grace with a pair of leather gloves. Don't mention it to the wife, but she has ambitions for Alex to marry into a higher class of rodent. Anyway, if all went well perhaps a ger-rat (or a rat-bil) would be of interest to your visitors, possibly?

Hoping to hear some good news, and best wishes for the New Year to you and yours and to the Grace and all his.

Yours respectably

RM Morello

PS: we could bring Al down in a picnic basket, with a carrot.

Park View Road
Ealing
London W5

28 January 2005

Ms Kate Harris
Archivist
Longleat House
Warminster
Wiltshire BA12 7NN

Dear Ms Harris

The Mrs gave me a great prod this morning re my letter to you of 4 Jan (special copy enclosed) and asked whether all was ok etc. She is angry that I stupidly referred therein to the Duke of Bath, who is in fact a Marquis and I wondered if that's why we've not heard.

I thought it poss it's cos some folk don't like Ital. persons like us but I don't think so and anyway we love animals like the Marquis.

Could we bring Alex down on 12 Feb (a Saturday) to arrange the intros refereed to?

We could take some fotos if that's ok and we'll bring some carrot cake (her sponges are like bricks).

Hoping to hear soon and thanking you.

Yours sincerely

RM Morello

website: www.lordbath.co.uk

VT/270

2nd February 2005

R M Morello Esq
Park View Road
Ealing
London
W5

Dear Mr Morello

Dr Kate Harris has passed to me your two letters of 4th January and 28th January which, being unaware of your previous correspondence with Lord Bath, confused her considerably!

His lordship has a very full day on Saturday 12th February – this being our official opening day for the season, but he hopes that you will enjoy your visit to us. Slightly concerned about young Alex being confined in a basket from London to Wiltshire with only a carrot for company. I would suggest that you discuss your plans for a gerbil/rat relationship with the staff at Pets Corner. We are slightly fearful that Alex may suffer at best rejection, at worst physical harm.

With his lordship's best wishes.

Yours sincerely

Viv Togg

Secretary to
The Marquess of Bath

cc: Dr Kate Harris

Stations: Westbury from Paddington; Warminster from Waterloo (change at Salisbury)
Motorways: M3 Exit 8; A303 past Andover towards Exeter; Exit for Warminster
M4 Exit 17 towards Chippenham; then towards Warminster

36

Park View Road
Ealing
London W5
4 October 2004

The Station Superintendent
London Underground Limited
Ealing Broadway Station
New Ealing Broadway
London W5 2NU   "urgent", please

Dear Sir

Yesterday (Sunday) I took my youngest, Rizzo (7), to Chessington Hamster Farm in Surrey. We bought two hamsters, one a little piebald fellow with different coloured eyes, and the other a sort of sandy beige colour, with a white bib.

Unfortunately on the return journey the family car (a Fiat 600, manufactured in 1962 and showing its age) broke down. So we got the train home, with the hamsters.

Finally, after some adventures the 4 of us reached Ealing Broadway station, and alighted onto a platform. I then noticed Rizzo's shoelace flapping around and told him to do it up at once if he didn't want to trip and fall under a 125 Express roaring through from Bristol. In kneeling down to do so, Rizzo dropped one of the hamster cages, which sprung open!

The next thing we saw was the tiny furry behind of one of our hamsters as the little rascal darted across the platform, flung itself off the edge and disappeared under a train, fortunately stationary at the time. We spent ages crawling around the platform edge trying to glimpse the rodent. I felt sure at one point I saw a pair of odd coloured eyes peering at me from under a carriage, but then nothing.

With a tearful Rizzo in tow I reported the position to a guard. I asked if the train could perhaps be lifted up to look underneath. He said he realised the urgency of the position, and that we must "write in" marking the letter "urgent" whereupon it would receive immediate attention, probably in about three weeks.

Mrs Morello is very angry at our negligence in this matter which is causing a lot of strain in the household. She feels he could be quite valuable with those eyes. Could you please not move any trains in or out of the station until we sort this out, or at least very very slowly so that the little chap has a chance of sprinting away.

Shall we fill in a form or something? Please let me know how we go forward. Strangely we feel very attached to the little chap even though we hardly got to know him properly.

The other hamster, Sandie, is fine. But seems lonely.

Yours sincerely

RM Morello

PS: could one of the station staff perhaps scatter some nuts and fruit under the trains each morning possibly, till we find Hammy?

PPS: if you have a station cat could it be lent urgently say to West Acton. Or North Ealing?

Park View Road
Ealing
London W5

16 November 2004

The Chief Executive
London Underground Limited
Head Office
55 Broadway
St James'
London SW1

Dear Sir

We recently had a small incident at Ealing Broadway station and hoped for some urgent attention. I raised the matter at once and was asked to write in to your station superintendent which I did at once. As instructed by a porter.

The family is awfully anxious not to have heard anything, and I have telephoned the station since but can't seem to get anyone. Rizzo and his friends at school are terribly upset.

Could you please look into and around the matter and advise me and the wife what's happening? We haven't seen a sign of the rodent since over 6 weeks or so.

Thanking you

Yours sincerely

RM Morello

RM Morello

PS: Doreen Travis (Mrs) was seeing her sister off at the station last Sunday and reckons she saw something that looks a bit like Hammy on Platform 3, possibly.

Transport for London

London Underground

TO/BT -675360

24 November 2004

Mr R M Morello
Park View Road
Ealing
London
W5

Tim O'Toole
Managing Director

London Underground
55 Broadway
London SW1H 0BD

www.tfl.gov.uk/tube

Dear Mr Morello

Thank you for your letter of 16 November enclosing a copy of the letter that you sent into Ealing Broadway station on 4 October.

I was extremely sorry to hear that you lost 'Hammy,' when he escaped from his cage, as you were passing through the station. It must have been a very traumatic experience, particularly for your son.

I am afraid that Ealing Broadway station is actually owned and operated by the National Rail company 'First Great Western Link', even though Underground trains serve the station. As a result, I cannot pass comment on the situation at the station, or on the best way that this issue can be resolved.

I have, therefore, forwarded on details of this case to 'First Great Western Link' so that they can assist you further. Should you need to contact them directly, their address is:

The Customer Relations Manager
First Great Western Link
Venture House
37 Blagrave St
Reading
RG1 1PZ

I am extremely sorry that I have not been able to assist you further with this. Please pass on my regards to Rizzo and I wish you all the best in your hunt for the hamster.

Yours sincerely

Registered office is as above.

Registered in England and Wales, Company number 1900907

London Underground Limited is a company controlled by a local authority within the meaning of Part V Local Government and Housing Act 1989. The controlling authority is Transport for London

MAYOR OF LONDON

Our Ref : 62626

Great Western Link
Customer Relations
Venture House
37 Blagrave Street
Reading RG1 1PZ

Mr R M Morello
Park View Road,
Ealing
London
W5

30 November 2004

Dear Mr Morello,

Thank you for your recent communication, which has been received by our office. Relevant information has been passed on to the station in question.

We feel very sorry for young Rizzo, and for the hamster involved. You can be assured that a clos eye will be kept on the area around the tracks for such a distinctive creature.

I hope your further travels with First Great Western Link are to your satisfaction, and less traumatic,

Yours sincerely,

Michael McGrath
Customer Relations

First Great Western Link Limited
Registered in England & Wales number 4804687
Milford House, 1 Milford Street, Swindon SN1 1HL

Park View Road
Ealing
London W5

11 October 2004

The Head Keeper
London Zoo
Regent's park
London NW1 4RY

Dear Sir

I am writing on behalf of Mrs Morello who has been helping the school class of our youngest, Rizzo (7), in their project on *"The Animal Kingdom"*. Each child in the class is writing a story with pictures, and each can ask questions which we have promised to pass to the Zoo, which we are hoping we can then all visit.

There has been huge interest in this both by children and parents. There were dozens of questions, so they all went into a hat and we had a sort of lucky draw overseen by Miss Tibbs, the class teacher, to select the first 10 out. These are the lucky questions that came out of the hat:

1 Dilip (aged 8): *Which can run the fastest, a cheetah or a giraffe?*

2 Choo (7): *Are elephants scared of mice?*

3 Daisy (6): *Do penguins have hooves?*

4 Kylie (6): *Once when mummy and daddy took me to the Isle of Wight I saw a little green parrot at the zoo riding a tiny bicycle. Can parrots ride big bikes when they grow up?*

5 Helena (7): *Do catfish have fur?*

6 Sophie (7): *Do hippos eat cheeseburgers?*

7 Delroy (8): *Are zebras black with white stripes, or white with black stripes?*

8 Billy (6): *How much poo does an elephant do?*

9 Olwen (7): *can sheep and goats have babies together?*

10 Anthony (6): *Do animals go to the zoo to be on holiday?*

Also Spyros (4) from Class 3 asks – *can we take the lions for a walk in Regents Park?*

Mrs Morello and I must apologise about some of the questions (especially Billy's, which Miss Tibbs told him several times was silly. We had both very much hoped it wouldn't come out of the hat).

41

Another question, from Olivia, was very long – in fact more like a story than a question, as she did not understand what she was meant to do. It was to do with whether chimpanzees wear clothes in the jungle, but then she listed lots and lots of different clothes, and got a bit confused. The question was about half a page long so although it got chosen from the hat Miss Tibbs hid it.

I am afraid the only question Rizzo had, after reading lots of books on animals, was *"is an ant the smallest thing in the world?"*, which we didn't bother to put in the hat.

I hope these questions are alright for someone at the zoo who knows about animals to answer in a special letter that can be read out at Morning Assembly. We all look forward to hearing from you, and seeing you sometime afterwards.

Yours sincerely

RM Morello

PS: Have you got lots of toilets at the zoo?

PATRON: H M THE QUEEN

The Zoological Society of London (ZSL), founded in 1826, is devoted
to achieving and promoting the worldwide conservation of animals
and their habitats.

LONDON ZOO
REGENT'S PARK LONDON NW1 4RY

www.zsl.org

Park View Road
Ealing
London W5

20th October 2004

Dear Children

Thank you for your wonderfully varied questions, you have all been doing a lot of thinking about The Animal Kingdom.

1) Dilip asked **which can run faster, a cheetah or a giraffe.**

A cheetah is the fastest land animal and can run up to 100km per hour!!! It can only do this in very short bursts (10 to 20 seconds) though before it overheats. Giraffes are very fast animals too, though and if they are frightened by something, they can go from a walk straight to a gallop and reach 50km per hour.

2) Choo wondered **if elephants are scared of mice.**

I asked one of our keepers about this and he said that elephants are sometimes scared of mice or anything else that is small and moves very fast. It is not really anything to do with mice, but something that suddenly touches them or runs by them and startles them.

3) Daisy asked **whether penguins have hooves.**

Penguins are of course birds, though they cannot fly. They are fantastic swimmers, darting and diving in the sea at terrific speeds. They have webbed feet like other water birds and these are situated at the base of their body (not in the middle, like say ducks). Their webbed feet are like rudders and help propel and steer the penguin through the water. So they do not have hooves, but strong webbed feet.

4) Kylie remembered seeing a **little green parrot at the zoo riding a tiny bike in the Isle of Wight and wondered if parrots can ride bigger bikes when they grow up.**

INSTITUTE OF ZOOLOGY
LONDON ZOO WHIPSNADE WILD ANIMAL PARK
The Zoological Society of London is a registered charity. No: 208728

First of all, there are lots of different kinds of parrots and they can be tiny like a budgie or really big like a macaw. So they do not all grow up to be big birds, and perhaps the one Kylie saw was fully grown

Secondly, at London Zoo we think it is very important that our animals show us their natural behaviour rather than doing tricks like riding a bike which is not very natural at all! Two of our green Winged Macaws, George and Mildred, often demonstrate their incredible skills such as cracking open a brazil nut in their beak at one go or using their beak and feet to climb upside down along ropes. In rainforest where these parrots come from, they would do these things naturally and it is wonderful to see how their bodies are specially adapted to their environment.

5) Helena asked **if cat fish have fur**.

No, cat fish do not have fur; they have skin or scales like other fish. There are lots of different kinds of cat fish which vary in size from 10cm to 5metres long! Some of them have a flattened head and a wide mouth which is surrounded by whisker like sensory barbels. These are used for touch and taste and actually look a bit like cat's whiskers which is how they got their name.

6) Sophie asked if **hippos like cheeseburgers**.

Hippos are almost totally vegetarian and they mainly graze on grass at night time. So I doubt that a hippo would want to eat a cheeseburger!

7) Delroy wondered if **zebras are black with white stripes or white with black stripes.**

Zebras are stunningly beautiful animals that are covered in black and white stripes; I do not think they are black with white stripes or white with black stripes!! There are different kinds of zebra and they do have slightly different patterning. For example, some types have a grey shadowing in-between the stripes.

8) Billy's question was **"How much poo does an elephant do?"**

Great question Billy! I spoke to one of our keepers who has worked here for over 30 years and he said that an adult African elephant poos enough in 24 hours to fill one and a half to two black dust bins.

9) Olwen asked **if sheep and goats can have babies together**.

The simple answer to this is no, they cannot have babies together because they are different species. So sheep will have babies with other sheep and goats with other goats.

10) Anthony asked **if animals go to the zoo to be on holiday**.

Animals at London Zoo are not on holiday but they do sometimes move to other zoos. For example if we have a family of monkeys then the son may grow up and want a wife (?) and so he may be moved to another zoo to be with a new female monkey.

So animals can move between zoos and sometimes they can even go to zoos in different countries. Zoos do not pay each other for the animals; it is all done for the best interest of the animals themselves.

11) I'm afraid that the answer to Spyros's question **'can we take the lions for a walk in Regent's Park?'** is a big NO!!

We have three lions at London Zoo, Abi, Ruchi and Lucifer and although they are used to seeing and being around people they are certainly not tame.

12) I would like to let Olivia know that **chimpanzees do not wear clothes** in the jungle; they don't need to as they have nice fur coats on anyway!

13) Finally Rizzo wanted to know if an **ant is the smallest thing in the world.** Ants are certainly very small and very strong too, but there are lots of things that are smaller than ants; there are some tiny creatures that we can only see using a microscope.

I hope that these answers will be helpful to you all and that you do visit the zoo to see some of them for your selves!

Kind regards,

Caroline Bellhouse
Schools Explainer

The Chief Executive
Blackpool Borough Council
PO Box 77
Town Hall
Blackpool FY1 1AD

Dear Sir

I and the family (Mrs Morello, Tosti (17), Amphora (14), Rizzo (7) and grannamama (88)) had a lovely holiday at Blackpool on Sea over the summer. We all thank you. We don't know much of England but we thought you do a super job with the town what with the Roman invasion spectaculars and other imaginary history events that never happened.

The only item that upset us apart from the doggie things dropping everywhere was an unpleasant incident on the Tuesday round the corner from the Cornetto Ice Cream Parlour when Mrs Morello (Rosetta) noticed Amphora had gone missing. We thought she was at the model village with Spencer, the lame collie from next door's at the Seafront Hotel. But we suddenly spotted her. She was in "discussions" (as Mrs M had to put it in front of little Rizzo) with a Scandinavian youth, who turned out to be from a language school up the town.

Amphora insisted she was only chatting to the boy. But as Rizzo said, why did she need to take her baseball cap off and wrap her arms round the youth's neck to have a chat?

I later noticed Rizzo on the promenade, throwing stones at a group of Swedish students down on the beach. I didn't stop him. He was very upset.

Anyway Mrs Morello wants to say something. On our last day we went onto the beach. The wife has very painful feet and has to wear special reinforced spongy-soft padded flip flops on the stones. When the time came to leave the beach we couldn't find one of them, and assumed it was in the bottom of the picnic basket. But we discovered that was a mistake back in London.

Could you advise if such a piece of footwear has been handed in at your office? If not could you or one of your staff perhaps pop down to the beach during lunchtime to have a look? You're bound to ask what it looks like! It's rather large (about size 8), pink with yellow flowers (daisies I think, could be pansies), or yellow with pink flowers. It was lost somewhere opposite the Blackpool Tower, or maybe further down towards Fylde possibly. (Spencer might have chewed a little bit off).

Thanks again for your help. Hoping to hear some good news soon.

Yours sincerely

RM Morello

PS: when looking please keep an eye out for a rather nice cigarette lighter I lost on the beach about the same time. It's one of those see through plastic ones. I found it on the promenade the previous day. It's definitely blue. Or perhaps yellow. I think it's got a bit of fuel left in it, possibly.

Our ref: BW T/x

19th October, 2004.

Mr. R.M. Morello,
Park View Road,
Ealing,
London W5.

Dear Mr. Morello,

Thank you for your letter addressed to the Chief Executive and passed on to my department for response.

I am sorry that Mrs. Morello lost one of her flip flops on the beach and note that you also lost a cigarette lighter. It is very unlikely that you will see either of these items again. I should explain that Blackpool's beaches have an ebb tide which means that the sea comes in and out twice a day. Unfortunately when something is lost on the beach, once the tide comes in it can be washed away for good or it might possibly end up in the Isle of Man. It's surprising, however, what we do find on our shoreline and you can be assured that we will keep an eye open and will let you know if either of these items return to Blackpool's beaches.

I hope that Tosti, Amphora and Rizzo enjoyed their visit to Blackpool, despite the unsavoury encounter with the Swedish students. It is regrettable that this happened and I can only hope that Rizzo has not been too traumatised by the incident.

I hope that all the family managed to return home to London none the worse for their trip to the North and indeed trust that you benefited from our renowned bracing sea air. Perhaps you will be able to visit our resort again on some future occasion when we will be delighted to offer you our Northern hospitality.

Best wishes to you and your family.

Yours sincerely,

Jane Seddon
Director of Tourism

Mrs Jane Seddon Head of Tourism | Tourism Division
1 Clifton Street Blackpool FY1 1LY

Printed on 100% recycled paper.

www.visitblackpool.com

 BITOA
The British Incoming Tour Operators Association

47

Park View Road
Ealing
London W5

13 October 2004

Mr M Wasilewski
The Park Manager
The Storeyard
Horseguards Approach
St James's Park
London SW1A 2BJ

Dear Sir

Green Park, London SW1

I wish to complain about something unpleasant in the Park. I spotted it at the weekend. It was quite near a bush.

By the entrance into the Park from Piccadilly there is a notice board with a large poster on it. The poster is headed "Pelicans in St James's Park". Below that, in the middle of the poster, is a photograph of a line of Old Age Pensioners lying around on deckchairs, gazing rather vacantly at a lake in front of them. Right beside the photograph of the old people it says:

"The first was introduced as a gift from the Russian Ambassador. The Park now has 5 of them in residence, one from Louisiana, and the others from Eastern Europe."

Then below that it says:

"They eat an astonishing 2 stones of whiting every day."!

I think these ridiculous comments, placed alongside a photo of old persons lolling about on deckchairs, are in very bad taste and are apparently a poor attempt at humour at the expense of elderly geriatrics. They should not appear in a Royal Park of HM Her Majesty.

They are also misleading. Whilst it is well known that elderly folk enjoy fish, it is wrong to stereotype them like this. For instance Mrs Morello's grandmother, Annunziata, certainly liked a piece of trout or haddock. Or a kipper. But she also ate porridge, cauliflower cheese and kedgeree. And boiled sweets.

Please would you confirm that this silly poster will be removed at once so as not to cause further offence or misunderstanding.

Yours sincerely

RM Morello

THE ROYAL PARKS

Mr R M Morello
Park View Road
Ealing
London
W5

10TH November 2004

Dear Mr Morello

The Green Park

I was sorry to learn that you were offended by our notices providing information on the resident pelicans of St James's Park.
The daily meal of whiting is very important to the birds and they certainly enjoy their fish supper.

I am delighted to hear that Mrs Morello's grandmother enjoyed a varied diet. Vaclav, pictured on the bench, is also fond of chips, particularly when offered by French schoolchildren. He has recently refined his tastes with the opening of our new restaurant and is apt to wander the terrace hoping for morsels of sea bass.

I think you may be a little harsh in describing the persons on the bench as geriatric, however I assure you that very few people loll in St James's Park. Or stare vacantly. There is too much to see and do. You should bring Mrs Morello.

Yours sincerely

Mark Wasilewski
Park Manager
St James's Park & The Green Park

END OF CORRESPONDENCE

St James's Park and The Green Park
St James's Park. The Park Office, The Storeyard, Horse Guards Approach, London SW1A 2BJ

Cakes and Fancies and allsorts

Park View Road
Ealing
London W5
21 October 2004

The Right Honorable the Lord Phillips of Worth Matravers
   - The Master of the Rolls
The Royal Courts of Justice
The Strand
London WC2

Dear Lord Phillips of Worth Matravers

      Morello's Cakes and Fancies

I write to you as Master of the Rolls, as a precautionary measure.

With a little help from Tyrone, Natasha and Rochelle (and Sammy on Tuesdays and some Thursdays) Mrs Morello and I run *Morellos' Cakes and Fancies*, a nice little bakery and pastries business *"catering for all your baking needs"*. We were established down in Devon in 1979, and have grown a little bit. Business is coming along nicely since the move up to London, and Mrs Morello's sidecar is being re-upholstered.

We are looking for a new logo for the sidecar and our vans (two). We already have a nice picture of a happy smiling pastry chef (that's me) but we need a new "strapline", as I think they're called, to go below it.

Would it be ok with you if our new logo, just under my face, read:

"RM Morello -- Master of the Rolls"

with a few buns scattered around the wording?

The colours would be sober and proper and the whole shebang absolutely completely professional ect. I wouldn't pass myself off as you or anything like that.

I would be most graciously request your consent to this as Mrs Morello is rather worried about the situation (she has painful feet as it is) and in fact is convinced I may be flung into prison, or something worse even.

I hope that's ok. As Derek from Speedy Sprayers is due round on Tuesday to price the job an answer in double-quick time would be a bonus. I enclose an SAE for assistants.

Yours most respectfully

RM Morello

PS: whilst writing we were just wondering if the Law Courts might like us to help out on the cakes and pastries side? Donuts and fancies come with or without jam.

ROYAL COURTS OF JUSTICE
STRAND
LONDON WC2A 2LL

22 October 2004

RM Morello Esq
Park View Road
Ealing
London W5

Dear Mr Morello,

Thank you for your letter of 21st October, seeking the Master of the Rolls
approval to use your new logo "RM Morello - Master of the Rolls" for your
bakery business.

Whilst I don't think the Master of the Rolls can actually grant or deny
permission to use his judicial title, he appreciates the courtesy of your letter,
and has no personal objection. In fact, we are aware of at least one other
bakery called "Master of the Rolls", this one being in Hampshire.

Whilst I foresee no problem with your using the term, you may wish to
Consider "Master of the rolls" (with a small "r") which may provide a clearer
distinction from the state title. This I leave to your discretion.

Finally, in reply to your postscript, I do not think the Royal courts needs help
with its supplies of patisserie, like most businesses we are contracted to a
single supplier.

ROBERT MUSGROVE
Private Secretary to the Master of the Rolls

PS. Perhaps you might send us a
photograph of the finished
product.

Cakes and Fancies and allsorts

Park View Road
Ealing
London W5
15 November 2004

Robert Musgrove Esq
Private Secretary to The Master of the Rolls
The Royal Courts of Justice
The Strand
London WC2 2LL

Dear Mr Musgrove

Morello's Cakes and Fancies

Thank you very much for your letter of 22 October with the comments about the buns and rolls etc and the go ahead for the title.

It must be annoying to you to know there's an impostor out in Hampshire or wherever but I suppose we could get round it by referring to RM Morello as the <u>Grand</u> Master of the Rolls! This would kill off two birds with one stick as it jumps over the other lot and shows we're different and better. It could even annoy them!

I understand the Master of the Rolls is a solicitor or even maybe a lawyer. If so could I ask him a question to do with the Bank of England? I could send him some cakes, or a flan.

Sorry about not understanding the patisserie supply position. Just to add we could serve you in court if you like, and put an extra fancy under the table for nibbling during court hearings etc. Should this be of interest.

Yours sincerely

RM Morello

ROYAL COURTS OF JUSTICE
STRAND
LONDON WC2A 2LL

Mr R M Morello   4 January 2005
Park View Road
Ealing
London
W5

Dear Mr Morello,

Re: Letter to the Master of the Rolls

Thank you for your letter dated 15th November 2004 regarding the use of the title of Master of the Rolls. Robert Musgrove has asked me to respond.

I am very sorry for the delay in responding to your query. Unfortunately the Master of the Rolls is unable to provide any advice on legal matters or comment on cases that are not before him. I am not sure what your query on the Bank of England may be, but if you require legal advice you may wish to contact your local Citizens Advice Bureau.

Thank you for your offer of patisseries but I regret we are unable to accept them.

Yours sincerely,

Monique Deletant
Assistant Private Secretary to the Master of the Rolls

END OF CORRESPONDENCE

Park View Road
Ealing
London W5

22 October 2004

Sir Peter Morris FRS FRCS
President
The Royal College of Surgeons of England
35-43 Lincoln's Inn Fields
London WC2A 3PE

Dear Sir

I write to you as the President of the Royal College of Surgeons, as a precautionary measure.

Recently I had to drop Mrs Morello (Rosetta) at the doctor's, where she was having her feet looked at. She has dropped arches, and a verruca which is playing up a real treat. She hobbles everywhere and looks like she's walking across hot coals wherever she goes.

Anyway the scene that greeted the eye in the patients' waiting area was one for sore eyes, (forget about sore feet!). Piles of people of all sorts and sizes lying around on top of each other, groaning and wheezing all over the place. A couple of patients had been waiting for attention for about 4 days and had brought a little gas stove with them etc. and some books. The receptionist (Doreen Template) told me I'd best leave the Mrs there, and that she'd sort her feet out if the doctor couldn't and come back on Thursday when she should be ready!

I have decided to start a little business at our holiday home near Frinton which is a surgery of my own. I'll be offering cheap but <u>rapid</u> surgical services, including amputations, maxillo-facial stuff and colonic irrigations. I've built a nice operating table from some bits of timber left over when we knocked down the old pigeon shed round the back. For marketing purposes I've set the table up in the front garden with a couple of big signs saying we kick off Tuesday week, so form an orderly queue etc. As luck has it we found some old Black and Decker gear in the shed which came up a treat when the rust was rubbed off, which should come in handy for heavy stuff like the bonework.

I haven't got any certificates or anything for this but we won't be doing tricky stuff like transplants or brain work to begin with. Anyway I'm getting some help from Ken Lomax at No. 43 who worked for a while at Sid's Butchers' in Paignton, and I've got experience working in a scrapyard.

We wondered if you might pop down for the opening, and maybe say a few words eg about how encouraged you are by another private initiative which is saving money and resources for the NHS etc? We're getting some booze in to ensure a lively kickoff, should that swing the decision.

I look forward to hearing. Thanks a lot.

Yours sincerely

RM Morello

PS: Please let me know if we need to fill in a form or something.

22 October 2004

The Chief Executive
Abbey National PLC
Baker Street
LONDON NW1 6XL

Dear Sir

Mrs Morello and I write to ask a little favour.

Our youngest Rizzo, (aged 7), is not at all intelligent. As well as coming last in most subjects at school he is also useless at games. However recently his auntie Donnatella (the wife's older sister, over from Sicily for a long weekend – we put her up in the old pigeon shed at the bottom of the back garden) kindly gave little Rizzo a piggy bank, with a few bob innit.

For reasons none of us can fathom Rizzo has since been inseparable from the ceramic hog, and in fact takes it everywhere with him, violently shaking it as he approaches anyone. Whilst this practice undoubtedly has it's testing moments we are delighted that the lad has at last shown an interest in something that could be useful to us, ie money.

In fact he and four local friends (Dwayne, Stompie, Bandol and Charlene) have formed a little group where they each put some money in to Hog each Saturday morning, after swimming. Rizzo told me they're called the Money Boys (though Charlene is in fact a girl, aged 8). They want to *"save up for a mortgage or other sensible financial product, like an index-linked pension"*, according to Stompie (7) who always now listens to Money Box on Radio 4, report his parents, Titus and Raylene.

Considering when I last saw Stompie 4 weeks ago, he was mooning himself at Mrs Frobisher from No. 23 and running away giggling whilst trying to pull his trousers up, things have certainly improved with Hog!

As the Hog is now full could the group open a little account with you? We thought it could be styled RIZZO HOG ACCOUNT (NO. 1)? They're a bit young and all a bit daft, so maybe instead it could be in the name of Rizzo's pet parrot Russell, who is 12? And maybe we could send you a few peanuts every month to put in a bag with the money?

These are just a few ideas. Please address your reply to the wife (Rosetta) as I am going into hospital next week for a rest. But the children are really keen to hear, and can all open their own accounts with you when they're older etc.

Best wishes

RM MOrello

abbey

Customer Satisfaction Centre
Abbey
PO Box 5129
Milton Keynes
MK9 2YN

Mr R M & Ms R Morello
Park View Road
Ealing
London
W5

Date:15 November 2004
Our Ref: 0173689A

Dear Mr & Mrs Morello

Thank you for your letter dated 22 October 2004, addressed to our Chief Executive. I've been asked to respond on his behalf. Please forgive the delay in replying.

I understand your youngest son, Rizzo and his friends, have a desire to save their money, and with Hog filling up quickly they need another way to do so. I have enclosed some leaflets for children's saving accounts which I hope you find useful. Should you wish to proceed with an application please call into any of our branches where they will gladly help you with advice and the opening of an account.

I have also arranged for a small gift to be sent to the children which I hope they'll enjoy. Thank you for taking the time to send in such a delightful letter.

Yours sincerely

Caroline Swan
Senior Customer Resolution Manager

END OF CORRESPONDENCE

To the Rizzo Hog kids,
Enjoy!
Best wishes,

Caroline Swan at Abbey

Abbey National plc, which is authorised and regulated by the Financial Services Authority only advises on its own Life Assurance, Pension, Mortgage and Collective Investment Scheme products. Abbey National Credit and Payment Services Ltd is an Appointed Representative of Abbey National plc which is authorised and regulated by the Financial Services Authority. Abbey National plc. Registered office: Abbey National House, 2 Triton Square, Regent's Place, London NWI 3AN. Registered number: 2294747. Registered in England. www.abbey.com

MISC 0337 NOV 04 DS

Park View Road
Ealing
London W5

22 October 2004

The Most Reverend and Right Honourable Dr David Hope KCVO
The Archbishop of Canterbury
Bishopsthorpe Palace
Bishopsthorpe
YORK YO23 2GE

Dear Reverend Archbishop

I write most respectfully but with some trepidation to make a small request. It is a little unusual perhaps but a matter to which we hope you may accede when you appreciate what motivates our letter.

Mrs Morello and I have three children, the youngest being Rizzo (7). He's been a thorn in our side for some time, coming last in most subjects at school and no good at all at sports. However the one thing that has caught his interest is animals – from every corner of that kingdom in fact. As a result and in the hope of settling him down, Mrs Morello (Rosetta) and I have bought him various little pets. But he's got into the annoying habit of claiming people he sees bear a resemblance to them. At school this has become an obsession, to the extent his class teacher has set a project whereby each child has to produce a photo of a family or neighbour's pet, and also of a friend or famous person they claim the animal resembles.

We had no such thing at school. But it has quite excited little Rizzo who at long last is able to involve himself in something which he feels he can do on the same terms as his classmates. His little gerbil Dandy (sold to us incidentally as Derek but urgently renamed) has produced a litter of 8 babies, now 2 weeks old with eyes open, and bits of fur. Rizzo saw you on television by chance and shouted out "*gebrils*" (he can't get the name quite right).

We would like to respectfully ask for your consent to Rizzo naming one of the little mites in your honour, we thought Wee Davie or perhaps Ebor? We appreciate this is an unusual request but hope you will feel able to agree given the exceptional circumstances on this occasion. Rizzo has a particular mite in mind, and we could send you a photograph of it if that would assist in the decision-making process? He would be thrilled if you were to agree!

Otherwise if it's not possible we can apply to someone else for help. Mrs Morello feels quite strongly that one of the other babies looks quite like Sir Cliff Richard.

Thank you so much for your attention to this small matter,

Yours sincerely

RM Morello (Mr)

THE
ARCHBISHOP
OF YORK

Bishopthorpe Palace
Bishopthorpe
York
YO23 2GE

www.bishopthorpepalace.co.uk

27 October 2004

Dear Mr Morello

Thank you for your letter of 22 October 2004.

First of all I am enormously flattered that you should address me as Archbishop of Canterbury bearing in mind that as Archbishop of York I am but 'Primate of England' rather than 'Primate of all England' – the style and title of the Archbishop of Canterbury.

I am delighted to hear that little Rizzo has at last found something in which he can enthusiastically involve himself at school. His teacher has obviously recognised his remarkable gifts by including the whole class in his obsession.

In view of what you write I would have no objection to Rizzo naming one of his 'gebrils' in my honour though given the tenor and tone of your letter I rather feel that 'Wee Davie' might be altogether more appropriate than 'Ebor'.

I shall be interested to learn of the response to any approach you might make to Sir Cliff Richard. Further given that you say in your letter that there is a litter of eight such babies, no doubt now excitedly awaiting their matches, it will be intriguing to know what other names you are currently approaching and what their response might be though no doubt all this will be revealed in due time.

Greetings and all good wishes.

Yours sincerely

+ ת ل Ebn:

Mr R M Morello
Park View Road
Ealing
London W5

Park View Road
Ealing
London W5

16 November 2004

The Most Reverend and Right Honourable Dr David Hope KCVO
The Archbishop of York!
Bishopsthorpe Palace
Bishopsthorpe
YORK YO23 2GE

Dear Reverend Archbishop

Thank you very much from the whole Morello family for your letter of 27 October regarding yourself and gerbils.

We were very excited to receive your letter with its red shield thing at the top and the other pieces around it and some keys etc. Even the postman said we had received a special letter as he shoved the post through the letterbox (though unfortunately he meant something unpleasant we didn't want from the gas board).

Mrs Morello (Rosetta) is very annoyed with me for getting your title all wrong and mixing up primates. Does it mean you're a bit less important than the Primate of Canterbury, or can you switch jobs with the other Primate depending where your living etc?

Is there a bit of England where the Primate of York can't go unless he asks the other one? We thought Wales might come into it possibly.

Anyway, we must thank you for agreeing to Rizzo's gerb being called "Ebor". He seems happy with his new name, and gave the Mrs a nip last Tuesday. Could we perhaps ask for a little photo of you to keep near Ebor's cage?

We wondered if you could come to tea and see the little mite. Perhaps Sunday 12 December, around 3pm possibly? We could meet you off the train at Ealing Broadway (Circle and District lines) unless you were coming in a carriage or something.

Yours most respectfully

RM Morello

RM Morello

PS Don't worry about a present for gerb, though a crunchy insect such as a stag beetle might be appreciated.

PPS Mrs M says she'll do a Victoria sponge, and we'll get in some Eccles cakes to remind you of Yorkshire.

THE ARCHBISHOP OF YORK

Bishopthorpe Palace
Bishopthorpe
York
YO23 2GE

www.bishopthorpepalace.co.uk

30 November 2004

Dear Mr Morello

Thank you for your further letter of 16 November.

I note that you write "we must thank you for agreeing to Rizzo's gerb being called "Ebor"". In fact I suggested that, given the nature of your request, I thought it better that you should call Rizzo's gerb "wee Davie" rather than "Ebor".

I enclose a small photograph which you request.

Unfortunately, given that my Sundays are already full with previous commitments – some people, of course, say the only day clergy work is Sunday! – I very regretfully will have to decline your kind invitation to tea.

Yours sincerely

Mr R M Morello
Park View Road
Ealing
London W5

Park View Road
Ealing
London W5

17 November 2004

The Head of Planning
Barking and Dagenham Borough Council
Town Hall
Barking IG11 7LU

Dear Sir

The Mrs and I have recently thought of buying a house in your locality and hope to move in soon. With the kids.

We wish to insert a bright red double decker bus in the roof so it's half sticking out. This is becos Mrs Morello (Rosetta) and I did our courting to begin with to Cliff Richard's movie *"Summer Holiday"* where he and Una Stubbs and others go on a holiday in such a bus, and because the wife thinks it would be romantic etc as a reminder of those happy times a few years back.

There's a massive loft with wasps and bats etc but we reckon we can actually get into the back of the bus and clamber up to the drivers seat and sit like in a rocket innit.

Please advise me if we have to fill in a special form or something. If it's easier we could insert a model shark in the roof instead which would be smaller than the bus but more like our situation nowadays. In case anyone flying overhead is worried we could paint on the roof *"This is not a real shark"* etc.

Thanks a lot for your help. Next year we might like to do a *"Goatscape"* in the back garden with little mountains etc and have some animals wondering around with horns etc to remind us of S Italy. And possibly some sheeps.

Looking forward to hearing soon,

Yours sincerely

RM Morello

61

The London Borough of
Barking & Dagenham

www.barking-dagenham.gov.uk

Mr R. M Morello
Park View Road
Ealing
London W5

www.barking-dagenham.gov.uk

24 Nov 2004

Dear Mr Morello

Insertion of double decker bus in roof

Reference is made to your letter dated 17 November in respect of the above proposal.

I have seen the film Summer Holiday on several occasions but I regret that I do not remember the scene where Cliff Richard parks the bus on top of a house. Perhaps this is in the directors cut and available only on DVD. However I am of the opinion that if you intend to use the bus as part of the living accommodation, it will require planning permission as it will project higher that the existing roof. I would suggest that the old Route master type would be preferable as you could position the open access adjacent to the loft hatch for east of entry to this accommodation and facilitate access to the drivers compartment in the front. The existing seats could then be used as a ladder. I should warn you however that not many of our houses would be structurally robust enough for this type of development and whilst the open back gives ease of entry it may fall foul of the Building Regulations requirements for fire escape from the bus. The positioning of a self closing fire door could be tricky. The relevant application forms can be downloaded from our web site.

The model shark idea I'm sure has been done elsewhere. For clarification purposes you may wish to paint 'This is a real bus' on your roof, for the sake of consistency, if you go with the bus idea.

With regard to your future plans for 'Goatscape', this may not require consent. Provided that your 'Alps' do not exceed 4m in height and do not cover more than 50% of the garden area, it could be classified as permitted development. Whilst this may be a bit limiting for the goats, I'm sure the sheep will be more than happy. Please be advised that this only applies if the sheep/goats are non profit as you are not allowed to run a business from a residential house without consent.

Beacon
Council
2003-2004
Transforming Secondary Education

INVESTORS IN PEOPLE

62

Thank you for your enquiry.

Yours sincerely

Tim Lewis
Development Control Manager
Planning and Transportation Division.

127 Ripple Road
Barking
IG11 7PB

Park View Road
Ealing
London W5

25 November 2004

The Commanding Officer
Territorial Army
- Combat and Infantry
Brock Barracks
Oxford Road
READING RG30 1HW

Dear Sir

Our eldest, Tosti (17), was recently befriended at college by two lads who are looking for some employment. The wife is of the opinion that they are rather super. She has asked me to write to ask a tiny favour on their behalf.

The two lads, Julian and Desmond (both 20), are very close friends. Tosti says they are shortly finishing a course called "*Fabric Design in lovely silks and satins*". The Mrs says they're charming boys, though both are rather sensitive, especially Desmond.

The lads would very much like to join the Territorial Army. They say they would love to do a variety of little jobs around the place, possibly cleaning up guns and boots, keeping the bedrooms nice and fresh and tidy and perhaps bringing the officers afternoon tea and cakes.

They would also love to arrange fresh flowers in the Mess and just keep everything nice and cosy for the men so they can relax at the end of a trying day marching around and fighting etc. They could also decorate the Christmas tree to be extra cheerful.

Julian and Desmond were wondering if you could arrange for them to meet some real soldiers in uniform so they can get a better idea of what goes on? The only thing that upsets them is raised voices or noise or swearing. Or smoking. Julian says any of these can irritate Desmond's complexion.

Perhaps you could let me know the position. Hoping for some good news for the boys. They're quite excited about the possibilities.

With best wishes

RM Morello

RM Morello

PS: If there's an interview or something, could they attend together in case either of them gets nervous?

PPS: Julian asks if the soldiers would mind calling him and Desmond by their personal nicknames, Daisy and Bunty.

Park View Road
Ealing
London W5

3 January 2005

The Guild of Professional English Butlers
PO Box 35
Hayling Island
PO11 0ZN

Dear Sir

The Mrs and I are planning a posh dinner party for March. Consequentially we need help as the wife isn't much use around the kitchen etc. We believe you are at the pinnacle in providing impeccable persons of discretion for such do's.

The lady of the manor asks if we could rent a gentleman butler with the following attributes: about 6 foot 2 inches tall, fine military bearing and gimlet eye, quite posh, and absolutely tip top in the whys and wherefores of social etiquetteness. In short, someone who shimmers and glides as if on castors.

Sitting down with us on the evening will be:

     The Reverend Maurice Trenchard DD, MA
     The Hon Henrietta le Scrope
     Jeremy Finch-Smith
     Derek Strongbow CBE and Mrs Della Strongbow
     Sir Neville and Lady Grindrod
     Herr Gunther and Lotte van Schleuss
     Chin Soo Wok
     Chin Chu Sock
     Mr and Mrs Isuzu Yamamoto (from No.26)
     Miss Scarlett Canteloupe
     Signor Vincenzo and Signora Calabrese
     Rocco Lambretta
     Jeff Stump

The Reverend Father is the most boring person I have ever met. He has no interests except cricket. So could your man be on top of Wisden's Almanack.

We shall be most eager to receive your terms for immediate perusal.

Yours sincerely

RM Morello

PS: could Mr Gent slip out into the back garden to feed our little Shetland pony, Thunderbolt, at about 8.30pm. Doubtless the lady of the manor ("call me madam"!) will be far too busy with the guests!

The Guild of Professional English Butlers

14th January, 2004.

Mr. R.M. Morello,
Park View Road,
Ealing,
LONDON, W5.

Dear Mr. Morello,

Thank you for your letter of the 3rd January which arrived this morning. Whilst the Guild does represent its member butlers in filling positions in some of the worlds most prestigious households, we rarely place butlers in temporary positions.

It sounds as if you are in for a very interesting dinner party with such a wide range of guests, not to mention Thunderbolt.

Perhaps the Reverend would be happy next to Jeff Stump so at least they would have some ground for conversation.

Isuzu Yamamoto, Rocco Lambretta and Lotte van Schleuss could discuss transportation over coffee.

Of course you should avoid serving cantaloupe melon as a starter; it might offend Scarlett especially if she is well endowed.

Likewise it may be best not to have anything stir-fried since it would involve the use of a wok and Chin Soo may get upset.

.....2.

Cont'd.

Whatever you do, do not serve any cider – the Strongbows will only gloat.

I think you will find that 'madam' will be too busy trying to find topics of conversation that interest Chin Chu, the Calabreses and Gunther to notice any lapses or shortcomings in your contribution to the social niceties of the evening.

Having been present at many such dinner parties I have found that often to relieve the boredom or stress it is best to escape to the garden and admire the stars taking care not to step into any deposits left by Thunderbolt.

I wish your dinner party every success.

Yours sincerely,

Robert Watson
Managing Director

(Dictated by Robert Watson and signed in his absence)

Park View Road
Ealing
London W5

3 January 2005

Sir Max Clifford
Max Clifford Associates
50 New Bond Street
London W1Y 98A

Dear Sir Max

I write at the request of the Mrs (Rosetta) with a cry for assistance. What follows might be likened to trying to turn a sow's ear into a silken purse.

Our daughter Amphora (14) is desperately keen to get on TV and dance around. Instead of exercising (she's hefty and should be burning off the crisps and Tangos she's always guzzling – she gets this off her mum) she lies around watching telly, and recently got obsessed with *"Come Strictly Dancing"* (or whatever it's called). As a result she now goes on and on about Natasha Koblinski and reckons she's got a great chance. The child's view is that she is a dead ringer for Natasha tho I can't see it, and although she has a rather fetching smile when it's forced out of her, I reckon that at 11 stone plus she's more akin to a porpoise with a weight problem.

Given the kid's natural disadvantages we thought you could assist somewhat in the public relations arena. Could we bring her in for you to survey? We can ensure a big fee when the little lady turns out as Best in Show one fine day.

Hoping for a favourable reply.

Many thanks

Yours respectfully

RM Morello

NO REPLY

Park View Road
Ealing
London W5

4 January 2005

Penguin Books
80 Strand
London WC2R ORL

Dear Sirs

Could you please assist me?

I am trying to find a book called *"Plums in History"* which I'm sure you published. It's a potted account of the influence of bottled fruit on world leaders from Tsar Nicholas the First - who never stepped on to the field of battle without a bottle or five of preserved apricots, and who had a first class record in combat - to the Emperor Napoleon, who ate mango slices at Waterloo, and lost as a direct consequence.

The other tome I am hunting down is *"Sexing Gorillas Made Easy"* by Daphne Philpott WRVS (this comes with a pair of reinforced gloves and a safety harness that hangs from the ceiling).

I'd like 4 Plums and a couple of Gorillas.

Hoping for a favourable reply.

Yours sincerely

RM Morello

PEARSON
Education

PEARSON CUSTOMER OPERATIONS
EDINBURGH GATE, HARLOW,
ESSEX CM20 2JE UNITED KINGDOM

unfortunatly These are not all titles
Sorry for any inconveniena

www.pearson.com

WITH COMPLIMENTS

Park View Road
Ealing
London W5

4 January 2005

The Chief Librarian
The British Library Reading Room
Euston Road
London NW1

Dear Sir or Madam

Hello! My name is Mr Morello.

Our youngest (Rizzo, 7) is very keen on libraries. He once read about unusual items found in library books such as fish bones, hairnets, biscuits and unpleasant rubber things. He would like to enquire how many of the following get found each year in the British Library Reading Room:

Umbrellas
Bowler hats
Animals (including fish)
Artificial limbs?

The lad also asks whether he could visit the library one Saturday after swimming to count the books, and to see how many you need to stack up to reach the ceiling. Could he also balance a few on his head?

The wife (Rosetta) enquires what happens to people who get locked in the Library overnight by misteak? Do they you have a special place they can make some Horlicks and then fall asleep, maybe near books about chemistry or physics, or stuff to do with Steve Davis (the snooker bloke)?

Hoping to hear soon. Saturday 22 January would be OK.

Yours sincerely

RM Morello

THE BRITISH LIBRARY

96 Euston Road
London
NW1 2DB

www.bl.uk

THE WORLD'S KNOWLEDGE

Mr RM Morello
Park View Road
Ealing
LONDON
W5

2 February 2005

Dear Mr Morello,

Thank you for your letter of 4 January, which was passed to me for reply.

Your letter asks how many unusual items are lost in the Library each year and disappointingly, we have found none of the items you mention. Our main item of lost property is the umbrella.

All public areas of the building are checked at closing time each day by our security team so no-one is ever locked in overnight.

You also ask how many books the Library holds; the collection is around 160 million items but it is difficult to be exact as we receive 44metres of new material each day. In terms of how many books would be in a stack that reached the ceiling, if we were in the front hall and used the Klencke book of maps, which is 2m tall, then we could stack 15 end on end.

Unfortunately we do not allow children in the reading rooms but you can see the Klenke book of maps in the lobby of the Maps Reading Room and also the other books of the King George III Library in the Kings Library Tower whenever the building is open.

We also host many school visits, please see the website for more details of our educational programmes at http://www.bllearning.co.uk/live/teachers/visit/.

Yours Sincerely

Tracey Henshaw
Head of Reading Room Operations

Tracey Henshaw
Head of Reading Room Operations

Park View Road
Ealing
London W5
6 January 2005

The Managing Director – Boden Central
Meridian West
Meridian Business Park
Leicester LE19 1PX

Dear Sir or Madam

My wife and I love your mail order catalogue - the Mrs spends a couple of hours a day
flicking through it - and would ask if you could consider the following gear for the next
edition:

1 **Pussy warmer:** a vent fitted to the top of the cat flap expels a tiny burst of hot air
   over pusscat as he/she/it pops in from the cold, leaving moggy warm, invigorated
   and puffed up. (Not suitable for hamsters).

2 **The Commuter's Revenge:** an umbrella which conceals fearsome blades of cold
   steel that flick out at menacing angles, enabling toffs in pinstripes to threaten
   instant evisceration when approached by speeding rollerbladers. Recover the
   initiative when surrounded by tourists, muggers and carol singers. Available in a
   range of attractive pastel shades.

3 **Disco Slippers:** funky bedroom slippers with a difference - these are pre-
   programmed to dance out the steps of the Top Ten Hit Parade at the "hit" of a
   button (one button on each toe). Useful for karaoke parties, and Darby and Joan
   evenings in twilight homes. 86 AA batteries (not provided).

4 **What the Hell was that?!** An alarm clock that, whatever time you set it to, goes
   off at colossal volume at 5am, discharging an enormous gush of ice cold water
   over the bed and its occupant(s). Great fun! Ideal for use on house guests.
   Deluxe version enables a sewage substitute. BMA approved. (Can cause heart
   attacks).

5 **Tortoise regulator:** a neat panel in fashionable *"Tortiflex"* sticks on the shell of
   the beast enabling you to monitor all it's vital organ functions round the clock. As
   seen on BBC's "Vetwatch" with Trudie Mostue and Sir Trevor Brooking.
   Underwater version available for turtles. Allow 28 days for delivery.

6 **The "Stuff It All In":** Say goodbye to wasted-hours-under-the-sofa-misery. No
   more grubbing around on the floor looking for bits and pieces and other crap with
   this handy "Lounge Organiser" to shove all your other organisers in that you got
   for Christmas. Plastic.

The wife is convinced these may do nicely in the festive market through your catalogue,
which as an expert she rates as best of the lot.

Looking forward to hearing. Thanking you

RM Morello

Boden

Mr R Morello
Park View Road
Ealing
London
W5

11th January 2005

Dear Mr Morello

Thank you for your recent and thought provoking letter. I am delighted to read that the Boden catalogue is so popular in your household!

As a committed 'Bodenite' you will no doubt be aware that we actively encourage our customers to get in touch and new ideas and suggestions are always welcome. It would, I think, be fair to say that your ideas are slightly different to those that we normally receive!

You may know that we dipped a toe in the homewares market with our mini-Boden catalogue and now have duvet sets and curtains in our range. At the risk of upsetting your wife, I have to say, that fabulous and inventive as your ideas sound, you are probably unlikely to see the Commuter's Revenge or the Tortoise Regulator in our Winter catalogue!

Your letter brightened up our day and raised a smile in the office, so thank you again for taking the time to don your inventors cap and share your ideas with us. You should, perhaps, contact the patent office to safeguard your future interests. Some of your ideas conjured up extremely vivid images, particularly the Disco Slippers. I can see my elderly mother putting those to good use!

Thank you again for your kind comments about Boden. Please keep the ideas coming!

With Kind Regards

Yours sincerely

Anne Devlin
Customer Service

Boden, Meridian West, Meridian Business Park, Leicester LE19 1PX

Boden is a trading name of J.P Boden & Co Ltd. Registered in England & Wales. Registration No. 2692601 Registered Address: Elliott House, Victoria Road, London NW10 6NY

Park View Road
Ealing
London W5

13 January 2005

TOP SECRETIVE
Mrs Anne Devlin
Customer Service
Boden
Meridian West
Meridian Business Park
Leicester
LE19 1PX

Dear Mrs Devlin

Thanks ever so for your letter of 11th inst. which I have discussed with the Mrs.who was quite excited and the kids.

I am very interested in the inventors cap idea you mention. Having tried it first on Tank, our bulldog pup, then on the wife (though I'd have preferred the other way round, for safety reasons)it will need quite a few wires, going in the back of the head thru' the brian and out of the ears, then with a little bell and a light on 2 (two) wobbly sticks poking over the forehead.

The light comes on if the brain has a good invention. And the bell tinkles for a duffer. Nothing at all happened for the wife but then I realised she wasn't plugged in! Batteries are hidden up the armpits. (Mains versions are poss, but could be tricky).

The wife struggled on the fitting (she's quite large anyway) but I'm trying it again now and then I'll send it over with the results for use on your mum. But <u>don't</u> overload her with the Disco Slippers (patent pending) at the same time. We had a near disaster at home: fancying a snack during Countdown the Mrs tried making a toasted cheese sandwich while wearing the *Inventor's Cap* and she had a short! There was a huge bang and a flash, and her drawers fell down!!

Don't mention the *Cap* to anyone at the moment (<u>especially</u> Trevor Baylis). Is there any chance you can squeeze it in for Xmas, maybe in the electricators section etc?

Meanwhile I'm on to the Patent Office like you said innit?

Yours sincelery

RM Morello

PS: the wife eats those mini-catalogues for breakfast, she's thru them in about 4.2 seconds.

Boden

Mr R Morello
Park View Road
Ealing
London
W5

17th January 2005

Dear Mr Morello

Thank you for your recent reply to my letter.

I will mention to Johnnie that perhaps our catalogues are too small, as your wife manages to get through them at such an alarmingly fast rate!

I did think after reading your letters that if your main source of earning an honest crust is not 'Inventor', then perhaps a literary career would be right up your street? Your narrative is extremely entertaining and descriptive.

Good luck with the Patent Office and thank you again for brightening up our day!

With kind regards

Yours sincerely

Anne Devlin
Customer Service

Boden, Meridian West, Meridian Business Park, Leicester LE19 1PX

Boden is a trading name of J.P Boden & Co Ltd. Registered in England & Wales. Registration No. 2692601 Registered Address: Boden House, Victoria Road, London NW10 6NY

Rt Hon Tony Blair Esq PC MP
10 Downing Street
London SW1

Dear Mr Blair

Our youngest (Rizzo, aged 7) is doing a project with his schoolmates called *"GOVERNING BRITAIN"*. They have to write a story, with pictures, to describe what it might be like being the Queen or the Prime Minister (like you are) or someone else important to do with government etc.

The kids are all very excited and they asked the teacher in charge of the project, Miss Tugg, if I would write to you with their questions. There were so many we had to draw a dozen out of a hat, so here goes:

1 **Neema (aged 5):** Dear Mr Blair, are you married to the Queen? If so, who is the Duke of Edinburgh?

2 **Leonard (7):** How do you become Prime Minister, because I want to have a go when I'm about 12.

3 **Pandora (6):** who is the most important, the Queen, Mr Blair or Geri Halliwell?

4 **Ronnie (7):** do you have to do homework all the time? I hate it. Do you like doing games, like rounders and jumping up and down?

5 **Primrose (4):** do you wear a Crown when you have your meetings?

6 **Kenton (8):** will Euan become Prime Minister when you die?

7 **Geoffrey (6):** do you have to shout at people all the time when you're Prime Minister?

8 **Jose (7):** can your dad ring in to say you're sick if you don't feel like getting up in the morning?

9 **Tony (5):** do you have to clean the windows at Buckingham Palace?

10 **Bobby (6):** have you got any pets at your house? We just stayed with a family in Belgium who had a baby crocodile in a glass tank that they used to take out for a run on Sundays. But it bit their granny's foot so they took it away somewhere.

11 **Topaz (5):** does anyone help you with the shopping?

12 **Kayley (7):** who is the best Prime Minister ever? Is it the one who was once a lady a long time ago?

Sorry about some of the questions being a bit silly but we would be so grateful if you had time to write to us, and we could read out the answers at Assembly one morning. With Big School present too.

Timothy had a nice little question, but he ran out of ink.

Thank you again.

Yours sincerely

RM Morello

PS: is it possible you could very kindly send a photo which we can display on the School Notice Board?

10 DOWNING STREET
LONDON SW1A 2AA

From the Direct Communications Unit

27 January 2005

Mr R M Morello
Park View Road
Ealing
London
W5

Dear Mr Morello

The Prime Minister has asked me to thank you for your letter dated 11 January 2005 about your son Rizzo and his classmates' school project entitled 'Governing Britain'.

I am afraid the many calls on Mr Blair's time will make it impossible for him to answer the children's questions personally. He was, however, pleased to hear about the project and was interested in the questions asked by the children.

Mr Blair has asked me to send the enclosed booklet about 10 Downing Street, together with information about his biography and 'favourite things'. He hopes that the children will find these interesting. They, along with the enclosed photograph, are sent with his best wishes.

Yours sincerely

S. James.

SUSAN JAMES

THE RT HON TONY BLAIR PC MP
PRIME MINISTER

Biographical data & a few of his 'favourite things'

NAME	-	Anthony Charles Lynton Blair
BIRTH DATE/PLACE & TIME	-	6 May 1953 EDINBURGH
HEIGHT	-	6ft 1"
EYES	-	blue
HAIR	-	brown
SHOE	-	10
COLLAR SIZE	-	16
	-	
CHEST	-	40-42"
WAIST	-	36"
FAMILY	-	Married to Cherie
	-	Sons: Euan
		Nicholas
		Leo
	-	Daughter: Kathryn
EDUCATION	-	Durham Choiristers School
		Fettes College, Edinburgh
		St John's College Oxford University
CUBS/SCOUTS	-	Cub
PLAY MUSICAL INSTRUMENT	-	Guitar
EMPLOYMENT	-	Barrister
DISTINCTIONS	-	Hon.D.Phil Hebrew University of Jerusalem
POLITICAL	-	First interest in politics/political career:- Interest in political/philosophical thought whilst at University
GREATEST INFLUENCE	-	Works of Scottish philosopher John MacMurray
CHARITIES	-	NSPCC

FAVOURITE JOURNEY	-	As a child train into Durham – past Durham Cathedral
FAVOURITE HOLIDAY VENUE(S)	-	Italy, France
HOW DO YOU LIKE TO SPEND CHRISTMAS	-	With family in constituency home

FAVOURITE THINGS -

Colour:	Red
Flower:	Rose
Recipe:	Pasta of any sort
Fruit:	Orange
Food:	Fish & Chips from local shop in constituency
	Asian: Naan bread, dahl, tandoori chicken
	Sweet: Liquorice
Drink:	Tea
Sandwich:	BLT
Breakfast:	Cereal: fruit and fibre
Hymn:	Jerusalem
Bible Passage:	St Mark IV
Hobbies:	Guitar playing
Music:	Beatles, Ezio, David Bowie, Bruce Springsteen, Simply Red
Sport:	Tennis, Football
Cricket team:	Co Durham
Football team:	Newcastle Utd
Books- Adult:	Sir Walter Scott's IVANHOE
Child:	Kidnapped & Treasure Island by Robert Louis Stevenson
Poetry:	The Soldier by Rupert Brooke
Ballet:	Nutcracker
Shakespeare:	Studied at school - Julius Caesar
Play:	An Ideal Husband – Oscar Wilde
Prayers:	A Psalm of the Sons of Korah Prayer by William Penn, 1624-91
TV prog:	Old black & white films
Films:	Casablanca & Schindler's List
Heroes:	Lloyd George, Mandela, Attlee
Wildflower:	Snowdrops & bluebells
Childs Toy:	Small red wooden train
School subject	English & History

Park View Road
Ealing
London W5

12 January 2005

Highlands of Scotland Tourist Board
Fairways Business Park
Deer Park Avenue
Livingston EH54 8AF

Dear Sir or Madam

The Mrs and I are doing a bit of a tour soon in her new motor she got being quite lucky what with the big sister's dogs in a race. We're coming down your way to Scotland though I don't know it as we've been living in Devon. And in Ealing.

I and the wife (Rosetta)would like to know a few things:

1 do you drive on the left or the right in Scotland. Or does it vary?

2 the wife wants to dress properly in case we meet anyone important like a VIP. (I reckon she means Sir Sean Connolly, who used to be a sexy actor). So the wife asks if the ladies wear skirts in Scotland, or is it just the gents?

3 are Scottish people romanticate like we Iti's are, or is it always so bloody cold (scuse the English!) that you can't get going etc? Everything looks freezing in the pictures so we wondered. The wife had a couple of sherries last night and was laughing on the sofa, I had to biff her with a cushion but she's pretty big anyway.

Hoping to hear soon. We love Scotland and your areas. Have you got a monster did I read?

Thanking you,

Yours sincerely

RMMorello

visit**scotland**.com
The Official Site of Scotland's National Tourism Board

9 January 2005

Mr R M Morello
Park View Road
Ealing
London
W5

Dear Mr Morello

Thank you for your recent enquiry that you sent to both the Scottish and Highlands Tourist Boards.

We would have liked to forward to you a selection of brochures to show you the different types of holiday you can experience in Scotland, however, your full postal code was omitted from your letters. If you can supply us with your post code by contacting us on 0845 22 55 121 any of our agents will be happy to assist you.

In response to your other questions:-

1. Yes, driving on the left hand side of the road applies to Scotland and all of the United Kingdom.

2. Ladies are more than welcome to wear skirts in Scotland. Kilts are normally only worn by men for social occasions such as weddings. Other than main tourist attractions or social events it is unusual to see a gentleman wearing a kilt.

3. Scottish people are very romantic as is the country itself. The cold weather that we often experience does not dampen our romantic nature. Scotland is also one of the most beautifully scenic countries in the world and whilst nice sunny weather brings out it's scenic beauty it can look sensational in most weather patterns.

There are rumours/myth that a monster exists in Loch Ness located in the Scottish Highlands south of Inverness. We can send you guides to this and any area once in receipt of your post code.

Once again, thank you for your enquiry, we look forward to hearing from you and wish you an enjoyable visit to Scotland.

Kind regards

Daniel Toal
Visitscotland.com

Fairways Business Park
Deer Park Avenue
Livingston
EH54 8AF Scotland

Email: info@visitscotland.com
Web: visitscotland.com

eTourism Limited is a company registered in Scotland
no. SC226890, trading as visitscotland.com

Park View Road
Ealing
London W5

12 January 2005

Head of Transport
Brighton and Hove City Council
Kings House
Grand Avenue
Hove BN3 2LS

Dear Sir or Madam

The wife recently bought a Fiat 600 (1965 model). It was in Exchange and Mart. She can't tell a motor from a barrel of monkeys! but anyway her biggest sister Donnatella had had a bit of luck on the racing dogs so she shelled out some of the winnings to the Mrs to repay for some liposuction fees that went a bit wrong anyway innit?

It's quite a nice pale blue colour, with some rust.

The thing is the jalopy's left hand drive, and the wife's a useless driver (from S. Italy). We're coming down your way next munth to see Stan and Peggy Stoddart in Rottingdean way. We love your areas!

Would it be OK for Mrs R to drive it on the RIGHT hand side of the road as long as she's sure there's nothing else around on the roads etc? and looks round corners. She'll go quite slowly at first until she picks up confidences, and wear her spectaculars etc at all times and please excuse the English. Maybe there's a form to fill in possibly?

Thanking you,

Yours sincerely

RMMorello

PS: Just for info, there's no reasoning with the wife. I gave up in about 1982. She's quite big anyway. Her late Dad Giacomo ("Jack", innit?) (Rest In Pieces) said it was the happiest day of his life when she got married. And left home.

Park View Road
Ealing
London W5

19 January 2005

Oliver Letwin Esq MP
Shadow Chancellor of the Exchequer
House of Commons
Westminster
London SW1A OAA

Dear Mr Letwin

The Deputy Prime Minister, (Mr J Prescott MP), has let it be known that he wishes for one of the newborn pups of our family's bull terrier Wendy, (which belongs to our youngest, Rizzo (7)), to be named after him. And in his honour.

We have received formal confirmation of this directive on official letterhead from Ms Della Georgeson, *Parliamentary Office Manager to the DPM,* which makes it law. So the wife, Rosetta, reckons observe this directive (New Labour) to the letter.

Little Rizzo, who is poor in class and useless at games, but adores animals, also has a pet gerbil Dandy which coincidentally has just produced a litter of 8 babies, now over 3 weeks old, with little pink eyes open, and bits of fur.

We are a big family, and don't know how to vote next time round. It could be quite close. High minded gestures may influence us.

Would you be happy for your name to go forward for adoption by one of the little furry mites? We would be happy to choose one of the robust ones, with strong legs. We thought Charles Kennedy could have a later choice when there's not much left in the litter.

If you are not agreeable perhaps we had better try the LibDems next. Or UKIP perhaps?

So we hope to hear from you, quite soon. The Marquis of Bath has already jumped in quickly to get one of the best ones. It might be wise to move fast.

Hoping everyday for a Conversative landslide come the general election!

Yours respectfully

RM Morello

PS: I should mention that Wendy had a different name when we bought her. Winston.

HOUSE OF COMMONS
LONDON SW1A 0AA

Mr R M Morello
Park View Road
London W5

26 January 2005

Dear Mr Morello

Oliver Letwin has asked me to thank you for your letter of 19 January in which you ask whether he would mind if one of your gerbils was named 'Oliver' in his honour.

He is happy that you should so, on the condition that J.Prescott, your bull terrier, is kept well away from his cage.

Yours sincerely

Mrs Elizabeth Campbell
Senior Researcher to
Rt Hon Oliver Letwin MP
Shadow Chancellor

END OF CORRESPONDENCE

Park View Road
Ealing
London W5

16 August 2005

Mr Chris O'Donnell
The Birdman
Warwick Castle
Warwickshire CV34 4QU

Dear Mr O'Donnell

I was astounded to read in the papers that Bandit, a 6 month old bespectacled owl which
you train at Warwick Castle, has been forced to wear L plates when he flies!

You are reported as saying that the bird bashes into things like trees and battlements when
he is in flight. Is this true sir? If so I hardly think it a valid reason to humiliate a poor
disadvantaged avian in public. It must be bad enough for him as it is having to wear
spectacles without adding to his sense of failure by kitting him out in colossal L plates, the
same size as those on a car – without any concession for his tiny stature.

Surely the answer is to adjust his spectacles a bit – owls' ears are notoriously small and
specs can easily slip. Or even to get him a new pair with correct lenses, making allowance
for an owl's phenomenal night time vision. Or feed him a few extra carrots.

Please don't dress up Bandit to look like an old car. You wouldn't fit a mouse up with
crutches etc. (although we had an aunt in Sicily who did put a rabbit in a small wheelchair
for a couple of weeks when it stubbed it's toe on a brick).

Anyway L plates certainly don't work. Despite having them strapp'd firmly on the Fiat
600, our second, Amphora (whose about 16), hit 3 walls in 10 minutes when I gave her her
first driving lesson.

As a lover of animales I look forward to hearing with appropriate reassurances.

Yours sincerely

RM Morello

PS: Our youngest, Rizzo (7), would really appreciate a picture of Bandit. He wants to nail
it on the inside of the pigeon shed so they don't relax too much.

✣ WARWICK CASTLE ✣

WARWICK   WARWICKSHIRE   CV34 4QU

RM Morello
Park View Road
Ealing
London W5

02 September 2005

Dear Sir/Madam,

Thank you for your recent letter regarding Bandit, our Spectacled Eagle Owl.

I'd like to reassure you that the 'L' plate worn by Bandit in the photographs was specially made and as such was much smaller than those used on cars. Bandit only wore the 'L' plate for the duration of the photo shoot, at all other times he is able to fly freely. The photo shoot was supervised by Chris O'Donnell, a falconer of 22 years experience, who ensured that Bandit was not distressed at any point.

As requested, please find enclosed a picture of Bandit (minus his 'L' plate!) for your son.

Thank you once again for taking the time to contact us.

Yours sincerely,

Jo Biggs
Communications Executive

✣
An Attraction in The Tussauds Group
Warwick Castle is a Division of Tussauds Attractions Limited. Registered Number 1284934 in England.
Registered Office York Court Allsop Place London NW1 5LR

Park View Road
Ealing
London W5

10 September 2005

Ms./Mr/Mrs Jo Biggs
Communications Executive
Warwick Castle
Warwickshire CV34 4QU

Dear M. Biggs

Re: the small bespectacled owl, Bandit

Many thank yous from the wife and me for your informatative letter of 2 Sept. with a pic of Bandit enclosed.

Having compered the pic with the one in the newspapers, it is the firm view of the whole Morello family – and of Ken Froggatt of no.86, who has kept budgies for forty eight years - that the creature looks far happier – and hugely relieved – without the L plates, rather than with. Bandit is visibly smiling, relaxed and at ease in the nude.

So we also all feel it would be kinder too if you could remove the bird's spectacles (maybe he could be kitted up with contract lenses?).

Please ask The Birdman (Mr O'Donnell) to lay off the torment of little Bandito!

Surely there is a moral dimension here?

Thanking you,

Yours sincerely

RM Morello

RM Morello (Signore)

Cc: The Bishop of Warwick

PS: could we come along to the Castle one Sunday to feed something nice to Bandit to cheer him up, eg a plumptious meecelet, or some vegetables? Looking forward to hearing.

park View Road
Ealing
London W5
10 September 2005

The Right Reverend John Stroyan
Bishop of Warwick
Warwick House
139 Kenilworth Road
COVENTRY CV4 7AP

Dear Your Eminence

Please may I and all the Morello family congratulate you and your wife on your
recent installation as the new Bishop of Warwick.

Although we Morellos are not members of the same church as yourselves and your
flock, we are great believers in building bridges and making amends for various
things that happened in past times with which I'm not familiar hundreds of years ago,
and which therefore wasn't my fault anyway.

My Lord, I must bring a distasteful matter to your attention involving the possible
unusual use of a small owl, right on your doorstep.

Poor Bandit, a tiny bespectacled owl presently of Warwick Castle, is the creature
concerned and who seems to be blameless in the matter. Yet he is being dressed up in
all manner of absurd and demeaning accoutrements, evidently for the enjoyment of
the locals. The poor little fellow has been forcibly kitted out with a pair of ill-fitting
spectacles, and even car L plates!

**No doubt if matters continue unabated he'll soon be wearing stabilisers, exhaust
pipes and ladies underwear!**

Didn't this sort of thing go out years ago?

I cannot establish who lives at Warwick Castle and who therefore may be organising
such behaviour, but hoping you may have some influence to wield, and be able to
swing into action straightaway. The wife (Rosetta) said she had only to glimpse your
picture to tell you were an animal lover!

Hoping to hear soon, for the sake of little Bandit.

Yours respectfully

RM Morello (Mr)

PS: Didn't we meet once, at Betty Johnson's whist drive in Leamington Spa?

THE BISHOP OF WARWICK
The Right Reverend John R A Stroyan

Warwick House
139 Kenilworth Road
Coventry CV4 7AP

4th October 2005

Mr R M Morello
Park View Road
Ealing
LONDON W5

Dear Mr Morello,

Thank you for your letters. I hope you don't mind, I have forwarded your letter to the Entertainments Manager at Warwick Castle and am awaiting a response. Incidentally, I have an Uncle Colin to whom I will refer as he is very interested in birds.

With warmest good wishes.

Yours sincerely,

† John Warwick

END OF CORRESPONDENCE

Park View Road

Ealing

London W5

10 September 2005

The Producer
"Songs of Praise"
BBC TV
Wood Lane
White City
London W12

Dear Sir

Mr Morello and I are the proprietors of Ealing Valley Sun Club. We are a small and friendly little group which meets, in the altogether (buff), on Wednesday evenings at the Acton Swimming Baths, and every weekend at the Methodist Hall on Ealing Common.

Most of us are Church of England worshippers (as well as sun worshippers!) although the club is inter-denominational. In fact we have representatives from all the main world religions. Visitors say we have a nice cosmopolitan feel to our members.

We all greatly admire *Songs of Praise*, which club members often watch at the Church Hall over tea and cakes. We would like to enquire whether you would agree to hold a naturist Songs of Praise at the Church Hall, with everyone in non-textile mode, just as God intended!

There is an amplitude of parking space at the hall for big lorries etc, and plenty of electrical sockets for lighting and the like.

We all look forward to hearing with some good news as the vicar, Reverend Hawthorn-Bennett, says he needs to make booking arrangements for the Hall.

Of course if the BBC does not approve of people of different faiths speaking to each other in an attempt to break down cultural barriers so as to establish a more harmonious world we expect everyone will understand.

Yours expectantly

Rosetta Morello (Mrs).

Religion & Ethics

<u>songsofpraise@bbc.co.uk</u>

Mrs Rosetta Morello
Park View Road
Ealing
London
W5

28 October 2005

Dear Mrs Morello,

Thanks for your letter and kind invitation to do a naturist Songs of Praise. This does not fit in to our editorial ambitions I am sorry to say but thank you for your interest in us.

Every Good Wish

Yours Sincerely

Michael Wakelin
Series Producer
Songs of Praise

INVESTOR IN PEOPLE

park View Road
Ealing
London W5

12 September 2005

The Managing Director
Andrex
Kimberly Clark
1 Tower View Road
Kings Hill
West Malling
Kent ME19 4HA

Dear Sir

May I raise a rather delicate issue with you, as the Head of one of the nation's most respected purveyors of toilet tissue?

Mrs Morello and I frequently exhibit our proud collection of hamsters and other rodents at Fanciers' Clubs throughout the country. These fancy shows are rather like a rodents' Crufts – and indeed twice we have taken Best of Show, both for our Peruvian Guinea Pig (1976) and then a fancy miniature rex gerbil in 1991.

Marks are awarded for poise , balance, shape and size of head and flanks ....and grooming.

Unfortunately several of the hamsters - of the very delicate Florentine strain - are exceptionally highly strung. By the time they hit the razzmatazz of the grandstand after a long drive they are extremely nervous – with sometimes disastrous consequences in the area of rear end personal hygiene. Yet a wrong move can wreck the chance of a coveted medallion.

Could you recommend the best toilet tissue to help keep the hindquarters in neat and tidy condition, sparing the little mites' modesty in public when surrounded by their peers?

Something very soft and forgiving would perhaps be ideal – **not** Izal for example. We both thought *"Wilkinsons' Fluffy Naturalle Bathroom Tissue"* sounded rather nice but early enquiries reveal it comes only in massive rolls.

A trial sample would be greatly appreciated – though only a tiny piece is needed commensurate with the target area, rather than a massive wad which might terrify the jumpy rodent.

Pastel shades would be an added bonus.

We are most grateful for any assistance you may be able to give in this matter before the new show season starts in early October.

Yours most appreciatively

RM Morello

Kimberly-Clark Europe

28 September 2005

Mr R M Morello
View Road
Ealing London
W5
UNITED KINGDOM

Dear Mr Morello,

Thank you for your recent letter regarding ANDREX® toilet tissue.

We are always pleased when consumers show interest in our products. In answer to your enquiry, we do not have a programme for sending product samples on request. We are sorry for any disappointment.

We appreciate your interest in our products and hope you will accept the enclosed vouchers with our compliments.

Gemma Traore
Consumer Services Department

Enclosure

001320253A

● Belgïe / Belgique Kimberly-Clark N.V/S.A. Consumentenservice / Service Consommateur Belgicastraat 13, B-1930 Zaventem Sociale Zetel / Siège social: Kimberly-Clark N.V/S.A. Adolf Stocletlaan 3, 2570 Duffel RPR 0404.048.451 ● Danmark Kimberly-Clark Nordic Operations, a branch of Kimberly-Clark B.V. Kundeservice Vadstrupvej 22 Bagsvaerd 2880 CVR 20 01 59 42 ● España Kimberly-Clark S.L. Servicio de Atención al Consumidor Juan Esplandiú 11-13 28007 Madrid T.I.N./C.I.F. B-20/002.671 ● France Kimberly-Clark S.N.C. Service Consommateur Siège social: 26 rue Armengaud 92210 Saint-Cloud RCS Nanterre 352 600 456 ● Nederland Kimberly-Clark B.V. Consumentenservice Pascalstraat 15, 6716 AZ Ede Gelderland K.V.K. te Arnhem nr. 09093177.0001 ● Portugal Kimberly-Clark Limitada Serviço de Atenção ao Consumidor Estrada de Alfragide, Km 1,5 Alfrapark - Edifício F, Piso 3 Norte 2610-008 Amadora Capital Social † 174,579,27 Conservatória Reg. Com. da Amadora 14166 ● UK / Rep. of Ireland Kimberly-Clark Limited Consumer Services Department 1 Tower View Kings Hill West Malling Kent ME19 4HA Reg. no. 308676

WEBSITE: www.kimberly-clark.com

Park View Road
Ealing
London W5
20 September 2005

Professor Simon Meyerson
Institute of Psychology
8 Willow Road
London NW3 1TJ

Dear Professor

I am writing regarding a matter which has caused profound disquiet throughout our household and which after many months of anguish and distress now calls for the most expert professional advice and intervention from a renowned specialist.

One sunny morning earlier this summer Mrs Morello (Rosetta) and our youngest Rizzo (7) were finishing the Saturday shop in Iceland (in Ealing Broadway – not Reykjavik!). They were just departing from the store when the wife espied a piece of paper, neatly folded, resting on the ground. Being of an inquisitive nature Mrs Morello at once laid down her burden and snatched up the item. Unfolding it she read the following, rendered in a precise and steady hand, on lined A4 paper:

> Charcoal brickettes
> Wood shavings
> Frankfurter sausages
> Prawns
> Mandarin segments
> Slug death
> Sauerkraut
> Carlsberg Export lager
> Kylie's Biggest Hits
> Tortoise

What appears – superficially - to be an innocent shopping list carelessly discarded by a fellow consumer surely on closer examination discloses far deeper concerns.

Being animal lovers we Morellos, and above all the wife, have agitated long and hard over the intervening months as to the fate of the poor tortoise, placed as it is in chilling juxtaposition with such ingredients.

We sensed that you, Sir, may be one of the few people with an insight into any possible derangement which could forestall some future improper use of a reptile. Any advice you may feel able to dispense will be received with enormous gratitude.

I feel bound to add that the list was penned in **green ink**.

Yours most sincerely

RM Morello (Mr)

Dear Mr. Morello & Family

It is possible that the tortoise was intended as a pet and as a clearer of garden 'pests' e.g. slugs.

Wish you all well and admire your concerns

All good wishes
Mr. Simon Meyerson

END OF CORRESPONDENCE

97

Park View Road
Ealing
London W5

23 September 2005

Ken Livingstone Esq
The Mayor of London
Greater London Authority
City Hall
The Queen's Walk
London SE1 2AA

Dear Mr Livingstone

We've just returned from a family trip to Bodiam Castle down Sussex way, near the sea.

The wife (Rosetta) noticed that the old codger who owned the place yonks ago got the King to give him a bit of paper called a "Licence to Crenellate". This meant he could do up the whole place like a fortress with a load of stone bits on top, to dodge behind if shot at with an arrow etc. And the King and his mates could come round anytime for whoopee etc.

Well, you've probably guessed it (I think there's a Mrs Livingstone or similar) – the wife wants to crenellate our place (above)! She reckons there could be a lot of aggro down the line in a few years what with lots of marauding Danes and Yorkshires and other foreigners to do with the London Olympics in 2020 or whatever.

As there's no King anymore now we're in the 20th Century etc I thought I'd try you as definitely the nearest thing to a Royal Highness as you give out licences for most things like dogs, pigeons, trains etc.

Hoping for a favourable reply. We'd like to put up some battlements too, and have an option on a moat with a drawbridge. And the Mrs would like a couple of murder holes over the front door like at Bodiam which we can drop things through on people who we don't want pressing the doorbell, such as the visiting Mormons. And Mrs O'Riordan from no.68.

Yours sincerely

RM Morello .

If you could sort it with a nice old bit of paper with curly roman bits at the top in olde writing like a double glazing guarantee I'd be in clover with the Mrs. I'll get you a beer or something or a couple of newts. Is there a form or something?

GREATER**LONDON**AUTHORITY

Public Liaison Unit

City Hall
The Queen's Walk
London SE1 2AA

Web: www.london.gov.uk

Our ref: MGLA300905-0771

R M Morello
Park View Road
Ealing
London
W5

Date: 06 October 2005

Dear R M Morello,

Thank you for your letter addressed to the Mayor of London, regarding your request for a "License to Crenellate". I have been asked to reply on the Mayor's behalf.

I am afraid that the Mayor is not in a position to offer this license, as this is something that falls outside of his governing remit. The Mayor and Greater London Authority form a strategic government for London, and do not issue licenses of this sort. You may wish to contact your local library or Ealing council for more information regarding this license, if it is still in effect.

If the license you require is of a royal nature, you may wish to contact Buckingham Palace. While you are correct to point out that a King does not currently lead England, a monarchy does still stand, and would be a closer match to that of the role of London Mayor. You may find more information regarding the "License to Crenellate" by contacting their Public Information Office directly. They can be reached at:

Public Information Officer
Buckingham Palace
London SW1A 1AA
Yours sincerely

I am sorry that the Mayor cannot be of further assistance in this matter.

Yours sincerely,

Tony Stewart
Public Liaison Officer

Email: mayor@london.gov.uk

Park View Road
Ealing
London W5
30 September 2005

The Head of Ladies' Fashion
River Island
Chelsea House
Westgate
London W5 1DR

Dear Madam or Sir

Could I respectfully request your professional advice as Head of the nation's leading fashion outfitters concerning a matter of contemporary dress?

The other evening our 2nd (Amphora, aged 14) had a gaggle of her "mates" round for a conflab before hitting the town (Ealing Broadway) to do some serious damage to the local funspots.

As the nest of vipers assembled (Lianne, Cherylene, Chardonnay, Sherita, Chantelle and Stacey) I could scarcely avoid noticing that each girl was wearing ultra tight hipster slacks, all of which sported a logo emblazoned across the back.

A closer look (difficult without arousing venomous looks) revealed to my alarm the following legends emblazoned, in turn, across the various rear ends:

PEACH, ANGEL, JEZEBEL, ATTITUDE, COCAINE and, across the rump of the particularly fat Stacey, **GORGEOUS!** *+ hideous*

To my dismay I then noticed that my own flesh and blood was about to take to the field of battle under the posterior slogan "MAYBE"!!

But the real horror was to come only upon the ladies' screeching departure from the scene and down the road, townward bound.

As quiet descended across the home I noticed the wife, Rosetta (48 inch hips, and 15 and a half stone) sitting, gazing silently into the hearth through thick spectacles, deeply engrossed in her own thoughts. The wife's expression turned gradually from faraway dreamy to a puckish and ghastly smirk. She leapt slowly to her two large feet, and announced in a challenging fashion and to my dismay that she too would buying such a pair of slacks, adding *"with a nice word on the back"*!!

May I ask – urgently – whether you have any more becoming garments for the traditional build of lady, with a strong emphasis on damage limitation? At present the only logo I can think of most congruous to the wife's circumstances (fundament) is "TITANIC". Or "TRAGEDY" perhaps.

Your earliest response would be appreciated, in order to avert a possible disaster. The wife reckons she's off to Trudgwick's first thing Saturday morning to try some on!
Yours sincerely   *Ladies' Department*

RM Morello (Mr)

PS: May I add that one of our budgies, Chuckie, fell of his perch and expired some minutes after the wife's announcement.

Chelsea House, Westgate, London W5 1DR   www.riverisland.com

6th October 2005

Mr RM Morello
Park View Road
Ealing
London
W5

Our Ref 2002/01

Dear Mr Morello,

We would like to thank you for your letter dated 30th September 2005.

We are always keen to hear about the views and experiences of our customers and would like to thank you for taking the time to share you experiences with us.

Sadly I am confident that we will be unable to satisfy your exact requirements on this occasion. However I would like to encourage you and Mrs Morello to visit our store stores frequently as new items arrive each week and we are confident that you will find something to your mutual satisfaction before long.

Our website is also updated weekly and offers a larger selection of styles and sizes than most of the stores. I would strongly recommend that you start your search there. You may also find something to help Amphora and 'The Vipers' recover from the demise of dear 'Chuckie'.

In the meantime please accept these vouchers as a gesture of our sincere thanks for writing us a wonderful letter that provided welcome relief to our day in the cut and thrust of the fashion retail world.

Yours sincerely,
On behalf of
River Island Clothing Co. Ltd

Jenna Smith
Customer Services Team

newlife action

River Island supports **The Birth Defects Foundation**
Health for babies - Hope for families. Registered charity no. 1001817
River Island Clothing Co. Ltd. Registered Office as above. Registered in England No. 636095

Park View Road
Ealing
London W5

30 September 2005

Mr David Ross MD
Consultant Plastic Surgeon
Suite 1
14 Queen Anne Street
London W1G 9LG

Dear Mr Ross

I and the wife's colleagues are planning ahead for her birthday coming up. We are hoping to treat her to something special this year - plastic surgery to reduce the size of her mouth - and would wish to entrust such a delicate consideration only to a leading practitioner in the field. I have a very favourable reference as to your abilities.

The wife has often admired herself in the mirror, but seems to recognise that some emendation could be beneficial. Mouth reduction to normal size in this particular case would be no trifling matter but would be a profitable venture and any improvement at all would be sincerely appreciated.

Could your rooms please submit your terms of business? We could get her in quickly should any vacancy arise at short notice.

By the by, do you do any general nip and tuck procedure which may attract a discount element for more comprehensive treatment? We had in mind a pinning back of the ears, preferably the two together, simultaneously.

This is a surprise gift, so please could you address your reply to me, not to Mrs Morello.

Yours sincerely

RM Morello

PS: Is there much discomfort in the procedure? Thank you.

W1
PLASTIC SURGERY

David Ross MD FRCS(Plast)

Consultant Plastic, Aesthetic and Reconstructive Surgeon

Practice Manager: Mrs Roz McGinty

5 October 2005

<u>Strictly Private & Confidential</u>
Mr R M Morello
Park View Road
Ealing
London
W5

Dear Mr Morello

Thank you for your letter of the 30th September enquiring as to aesthetic surgery for your wife as an impending birthday present. From your letter it appears that your wife is not aware of your request. Therefore I think in the first instance it would be important to emphasise that your wife would need to seek a formal consultation so that I may get an opportunity to examine her and assess exactly what the problem is and then discuss any possible corrective procedures.

It would obviously be essential that I do get to meet her long before any surgery is contemplated so that I may formally examine her and be able to discuss any surgical solution. It would then be important that your wife had a period of time to contemplate matters so that she may fully appreciate the procedure itself and the attendant risks and recovery. With this in mind I wonder whether you would kindly contact my secretary so that we may make a suitable appointment

With kind regards

Yours sincerely

[signature]

Mr David Ross MD FRCS (Plast)
Consultant Plastic, Aesthetic and Reconstructive Surgeon

END OF CORRESPONDENCE

W1
PLASTIC SURGERY

Correspondence Address:
Suite 1
14 Queen Anne Street
London W1G 9LG

Plastic Surgery W1 Ltd
Registered office: 46 Moray Place Edinburgh
Registered No: 234223 Scotland

NHS Consultancy:
Dept of Plastic Surgery
St Thomas' Hospital
London SE1 7EH

Park View Road
Ealing
London W5

1 October 2005

Ms Patricia Hewitt
Secretary of State for Health
Richmond House
79 Whitehall
London SW1

Dear Secretary of State

I believe I read somewhere last week that **the NHS uses on average 38% less anaesthetic on surgical procedures than where you are operated on privately.**

This is a shocking statistic! Surely relative consciousness is a definite disadvantage with some sorts of operations!? I would have thought that any differential of anaesthesia between public and private patients over about 25% would be unacceptable, after making allowance for the fact that NHS patients aren't paying anything for their op.

Does the NHS have any plans to reduce the figure down a bit over say the next 10 to 15 years, say to 36% or 35 possibly? This is one area where a target could make good sense.

Mrs Morello (Rosetta) is due to have her corns redacted on the National Health in a couple of weeks. She is highly apprehensive and is of a surprisingly large frame anyway. Her concern centres on the thought that the gas might run out or the jab be diluted.

Would it be wrong to reassure her in this matter before the event? If I cannot do so I shall assume that NHS patients will soon be asked to attend hospital only if accompanied by their own bed and medical staff!

This surely can't be the way to run a public service in the 20th century? Will the DoH be taking up a robust position with regards to this one?

I shall be most grateful for your reply before Mrs M falls under the knife a week on Friday.

Yours sincerely

RM Morello (Mr)

Department of Health

Richmond House
79 Whitehall
London
SW1A 2NS

Our ref: TO00036848

Mr R Morello
Park View Road
Ealing
London W5

14 October 2005

Dear Mr Morello,

Thank you for your letter of 1 October to Patricia Hewitt about anaesthetic. As you will appreciate, Mrs Hewitt receives a large amount of correspondence and is unable to reply to all her mail personally. Your letter has been passed to me for reply.

I would reject any assertion that there is a policy of inadequate doses of anaesthetic. All anaesthetics are used in accordance with the highest professional standards and would certainly not be used in such a way that would put some patients at a *definite disadvantage with some sorts of operations*.

I can thus reassure Mrs Morello that her anaesthetist will take into account all of her individual circumstances to ensure that she suffers no pain during the procedure.

I hope this information is helpful.

Yours sincerely

Keith Roberts
Customer Service Centre

UK
PRESIDENCY
OF THE EU
2005

Park View Road
Ealing
London W5

12 October 2005

The Senior Partner
Winters - Accountants
29 Ludgate Hill
London EC4M 7JE

Dear Sir

I worked for Winters from 1987 till 1993 and had a thoroughly pleasant time at one of the best and mightiest accountancy firms.

I believe I may have left a banana in my desk when leaving. Could I collect it please?

I'll pop round about 2pm on 19th October if that's ok?

Many thanks

Yours sincerely

RM Morello (Mr)

PS: Mrs M would like to come too but her feet (bunions) are playing her up something rotten.

CHARTERED ACCOUNTANTS
TAX CONSULTANTS
BUSINESS ADVISERS

29 Ludgate Hill, London EC4M 7JE

Mr R M Morello   AAM Staff
Park View Road
Ealing
London W5   17 October 2005

Dear Mr Morello

Thank you for your letter of 12 October addressed to our Senior Partner that has been passed to me as I was the staff partner during your time with us. I can now reply as follows.

I did not immediately recall you working here at Winters until reading your reference to your wife's feet. I do remember Maureen Town of the same vintage as yourself who worked in our tax department who as well as being a martyr to her feet was very much looking forward to becoming Mo Morello. Very belated congratulations to you both!

Now to the matter in hand. On receipt of your letter I immediately instigated a search for the banana you referred to. However I must point out we have had two refurbishments of our offices since your departure to accommodate business acquisitions we have made and I can no longer be sure which was your particular desk. This of itself would not be a problem except the search revealed no less than seven unclaimed bananas (not to mention three cucumbers, a marrow, several apples and pears, and a bag of sprouts).

Therefore to assist in identifying your own banana I wonder if you can recall any distinguishing marks. I must ask you to be quite specific in this regard as nearly all the bananas found are yellow and slightly curved. That having been said, it does seem a few that I believe to be the older ones have taken on a noticeably darker hue with the passage of time and if you could recall in which year you placed the banana in your desk this may also help to narrow down the list of suspects.

We could of course carry out a banana identity parade for you but I am sure you will understand we should not allow bananas to be claimed willy-nilly by any Tom, Dick or Harry as, if the rightful owner was then to surface, this could lead to a very distressing situation indeed.

Can I therefore suggest you reply to this letter with further details before we arrange any visit for you to the offices.

Meanwhile, very best wishes to yourself and Mo.

Yours sincerely

ANDREW MOLE

Clive Bailey FCA · Shabbir Merali FCA · Andrew Mole FCA · Kevin Fisher ATII · Chris Morgans ACA · Philip Clark FCA · Melvyn Yude FAPA
Mel White FCA ATII · Ian Warwick FCCA · Janet Taylor

Registered to carry on audit work and regulated for a range of investment business activities by The Institute of Chartered Accountants in England and Wales

The UK 200 Group   Winters   International Association
                          Chartered Accountants   of Practising Accountants

Park View Road
Ealing
London W5

12 October 2005

Lord Falconer of Thoroton
The Lord Hi Chancellor
The Department of Constitututional Affairs
Selborne House
54-60 Victoria Street
London SW1E 6QW

Dear Lord Hi Chancellor Sir

I understand you have recently passed a law whereby you can marry your own mother-in-law, and this applies not just to you.

May I respectfully point out that it is not always a good idea to marry your mother-in-law, especially if you're me. So I'm hoping this law only applies to some people not everyone (including me).

I cannot tell you how much I do **not** wish to marry my mother-in-law. I cannot over-emphrasise this. I can't send you a picture of the old bird anyway which could easily be connotated as a malicious communication.

Could you please clarify the position on this law as the wife's mamma is kipping with us at present here? The other night when the wife was out playing 10 pin bowls down the Acton Empire with the Ladies' Stoats' Club, the monster-in-law put on some Mantovani and candles and tried getting me sloshed on Valpolicella from Budgen's. **I think she had what's what in mind! The only good thing is she makes the Mrs. look quite nice when you've had a few innit?**

Yours sincerely

RM Morello (Mr)

Cc: Miss Claire Rayner

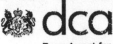

**Department for
Constitutional Affairs**
Justice, rights and democracy

Daniel Flury
Private Secretary to
The Rt Hon Lord Falconer of Thoroton
Selborne House
54 Victoria Street
London SW1E 6QW

www.dca.gov.uk

Mr RM Morello
Park View Road
Ealing
London
W5

2M.   October 2005

Dear Mr Morello

Thank you for you recent letters regarding the situation between yourself and your mother-in-law.

Although the recent judgement made by the European Court of Human Rights does apply to all European citizens, you should in no way feel compelled to marry your mother-in-law.

Even though your domestic arrangements sound rather complex, they are, of course, entirely your own business.

Yours sincerely

Daniel Flury
Private Secretary to the Lord Chancellor

Park View Road
Ealing
London
19 November 2005

Mrs T. Rowell
The Old English Goat Society
West Chapel House
Chapel le Dale
Ingleton
Via Carnforth LA6 3JG

Dear Mrs Rowell

Could I request some advice from you, as a highly respected old goat club?

We have several goats, who wander cheerfully around the back garden, eating dandelions and various things, climbing the trees, attacking each other etc. But Hermann, our brown and white billy, seems to have become deeply depressed.

Every Saturday evening just as the music begins to announce the start of *"Lottery Sweep"* on BBC1, Hermann wanders slowly from the garden into the lounge and stands, totally still, about 2 feet (75 cms.) from the TV screen, staring at it. Then, as soon as Dale Winton comes on, Hermann starts going to the toilet (biggies). This continues, almost non-stop, until Dale says goodnight and cheerio. Then, very slowly, Hermann backs away from the screen and returns silently into the garden, where he stands staring blankly at the fence. Much later he falls over in the nettles and curls up.

Is this viewing habit just becos Hermann has a very low IQ? Anyway he's never bought a ticquet, so it seems pointless to tune in. Perhaps he needs a lady goat possibly? All the others are happy – Enoch, Constance (Mrs Enoch), Patrick and Rubrik.

Hermann used to be such a happy-go-lucky, carefree goat. He'd hang around the front garden where every morning he would butt the postman Mr Hampshire, and kick him in the shins a bit. But postie's retired hurt (legs etc) – he caught one in the testimonials a while back, and gave up. Hermann used to enjoy injuring him slightly. Now he seems so depressed all the time. He's even gone off his Weetabix and brussels.

What can we do? Could we ask the Lotto producer to move Dale on, eg to Panorama or something? Or maybe we should get in Sky TV - the wife reckons they have quite nice wildlife programmes, with pandas, crocs etc. And gorillas.

Any advices you might supply would be most appreciated. We could bring Hermann down to Devon (where he and we used to live originally) if an inspection might assist, possibly? Many thanks for your assistance.
Yours sincerely

RMMorello (Mr)

PS: the wife (Rosetta) has tugged his tail quite hard a few times to cheer him up. But then he seems to go even more.

PPS: do you know any really good carpet cleaner?

West Chapel House
Chapel-le-Dale
Ingleton
Via Carnforth
LA6 3JG

28 November '05

Dear Mr Morello,

Thank you for your letter of the 19th which I have forwarded to the editor of our newsletter for consideration.

I am afraid your story brings "Star Trek" comes to mind: to paraphrase, these are goats, Jim, but not as we know them.

My only suggestion is that you might install some doors or gates. An alternative might be to upgrade your standard of TV shows which you watch...

Yours sincerely

Thelma Rawell.
Secretary, O.E.G.S.

Mr Adam Crozier
Chief Executive
The Royal Mail
148 Old Street
London EC1V 9HQ

Dear Mr Crozier

I write to you as the country's top postie, with a small plea.

One of our favourite goats, a quite rare pygmy Boer goat called Hermann, is dreadfully upset. He can't come to terms with the retirement (through injury) of our postman Mr Hampshire a couple of weeks ago. He really used to enjoy butting and ramming Mr H slightly as he came up the garden with the morning's post. Perhaps his finest hour was tipping Mr Hampshire (who made the mistake of trying to swerve past him wielding a broomstick) into a bed of dahlias. He then grabbed the postbag, and had half eaten about 11 letters and a piece of postal order when we wrenched the bag away.

Now Hermann seems so hangdog and morose. All he wants to do is watch TV, particularly *Lottery Sweep* with Dale Winton, and old episodes of *Rawhide* on Channel Five. He stands for hours facing the television with glazed eyes, in complete silence, whilst making a mess on the carpet.

Could you please see if Mr Hampshire might return? He's only c 63 years old and although quite thin and a bit slow with that limp, he's very popular locally what with his antics trying to avoid Hermann, and running away shouting etc. There should be a few more years in him. Maybe you could get him some running shoes or something.

We've had a load of different postmen since who I think are temporaries, and although it's interesting to receive next door's post all the time, these temp posties are of no interest to Hermann, whose always on the lookout for Mr H. When he sees a temp arriving instead he just walks slowly away, and lies down under the rosebush groaning.

Geoff Cundell (at no.36) reckons if things don't improve, he'd make a fine curry. I think he was talking about Hermann, not Mr Hampshire.

Hoping to hear soon with a favourable reply.

Yours respectfully

RM Morello (Mr)

PS: are you still doing the FA job as well? It would be funny if you had to deliver the post to your other job. Then it wouldn't matter if you couldn't get up in the morning as you'd have no post to open in your office anyway.

Date: 1 December 2005

Our Ref: **1-1643891671**

Mr R Morello
Park View Road
LONDON
W5

Dear Mr Morello

Thank you for your letter of 19 November to Mr Adam Crozier, Chief Executive of Royal Mail, requesting the return of your old postman and also about the problems you have had with delivery of mail to your address.

May I begin by offering my sincere apologies for any concern and inconvenience you have been caused by the misdeliveries you have received. I fully appreciate how important it is for our customers to have confidence in our ability to ensure a high standard of service at all times and I realise the anxiety that is caused when this does not happen.

When I received your letter, I contacted Mr David Holland, the Manager of Ealing Delivery Office. He informed me you have a regular postman, who delivers your mail for five weeks in six and that the same relief officer delivers your mail during his weeks off. He was concerned to hear of the problems you mentioned, however without dates of misdelivery or the envelopes in question, he was unfortunately unable to make further enquiries. If you receive any more misdelivered letters, please forward them to me and I will be happy to investigate this matter further.

If I may turn to your enquiry concerning Mr Hampshire. Mr Holland told me that unfortunately, Mr Hampshire left Royal Mail employment a number of years ago. I very much regret any disappointment that this will cause.

I would like to apologise once again for any inconvenience you have been caused. I hope your future dealings with us are of a more positive nature and, if I may be of any further assistance in this matter, please do not hesitate to contact me and I will be more than happy to help.

Yours sincerely

Tim Evans
Royal Mail Headquarters

5th Floor, 148 Old Street, LONDON EC1V 9HQ

Park View Road
Ealing
London W5

5 December 2005

Mr Timothy Evans
The Royal Mail
148 Old Street
London EC1V 9HQ

Dear Mr Evans

We've just received your epistle of the 1st December (ref 1-1643891671), which the wife noted at once arrived by the hand of yet another **temporary** postman. This was considered by the Mrs a somewhat insensitive riposte to our letter of 19 Nov. given the plight of poor Hermann, whom we noted didn't even get a mention in your letter.

It is some consolation that we received a load of post addressed to our neighbours, so thanks for that anyway. (the wife said she had no idea Mrs Simkin is seeing the tennis instructor from Pitshanger Park courts, only two months after Neville left her).

Hermann seems even more depressed than before since your letter arrived. I note Mr Crozier's assistant Mr Holland claims that Ken Hampshire left the Post Office *"a number of years ago"*. **Well that's odd is all the wife can say as we've seen him in postie's outfit within the past three weeks down at Hanwell leaning on a letter box rubbing his dodgy leg that Hermann got that time when Mr H copped it in the shin.**

Would the PO/Royal Mail mind if we put up a little statue to Mr Hampshire in the front garden? This would remind Hermann of old times, and maybe get him out of himself a bit. He's terribly upset. Would Mr Crozier attend to do the unveiling? He could have some cakes.

Could you advise by 16 December as we need to send out the invitatations.

Meanwhile I shall certainly ensure that any envelopes we don't receive are forwarded to you to investigate, so many thanks for the suggestion, though this may prove quite difficult.

Yours sincerely

RM Morello (Mr)

Date: 20 December 2005

Our Ref: **1-1661547083**

Mr R Morello
Park View Road
LONDON
W5

Dear Mr Morello

Thank you for your letter of 5 December, about your old postman and problems you have experienced with delivery of mail.

I am sorry to hear of the inconvenience you have suffered. We do our best to provide our customers with the service they require and it is always disappointing when we are unable to do so.

If I may first clarify, Mr Holland, the Manager at Ealing Delivery Office, informed me he joined the Royal Mail twenty years ago and Mr Hampshire had left before then. I am pleased you felt Mr Hampshire provided good service and I am sorry for any disappointment you or Herman feel because he is no longer on your delivery round.

In my previous letter, I advised that if you received misdelivered items, you might wish to send them to me, to help with my investigations. I apologise if you have had further problems of this nature and in response to this, I contacted Mr Craig Chase, the reserve Manager at Ealing Delivery Office. Mr Chase said on the day you reported receiving misdelivered mail, the regular postman was not on duty. He advised the officer who delivered your mail on that day to take more care, although he added they have received some mail for you addressed to Park View Road.

May I once again apologise for any inconvenience or disappointment that you or any members of your household have suffered. If you require any further help or clarification as a result of this matter, please do not hesitate to contact me again.

Yours sincerely

Tim Evans
Royal Mail Headquarters

5th Floor, 148 Old Street, LONDON EC1V 9HQ

Park View Road
Ealing
London W5
20 November 2005

Sandy Nairne
Director
The National Portrait Gallery
St Martin's Place
London WC2H 0HE

Dear Sir or Madam

I would like to congratulate the National Portrait Gallery on a marvellous collection of pics and a splendid gift shop too.

A few years back the wife's mamma gave the Mrs a portrait of herself which is in fact bloody hideous (apologies for the loose tongue). It's done in ghastly livid reds and blacks slapped on in great strokes and weals, with angular and geometric slashes. A dark and hideous gloom pervades the end result. The overall effect is one of ineffable hopelessness – with the awful features of the mother-in-law's face peering out of the gloom with a menacing smirk.

The only concession to light is a flash of white near the top right hand corner. Lengthy speculation by family and guests clapping eyes on the work conclude that this may be the old dear's false teeth sailing through the air: in later years she has been inclined to hurl anything within immediate reach at those entering her bedroom for whatever reason. So the flash could equally be a knife, fork or glass of water, all of which along with boots and smoking pipes and transistor radios have been aimed at bedroom visitors.

Anyone who has known the old bird would immediately recognise the artist's fidelity to the observed world, a faithful exponent of the school of realism, of things as they truly are rather than as we would wish them to be. So you might think there is a ready home for such a masterpiece at the Tate Modern, or over the Saatchis' mantelpiece in North Hampstead.

However we heard that the NPG is rather short of exhibits, and I wondered if you may like to have this ouevre. The wife (Rosetta) feels it may be worth a little something. But I feel it would be a nice gesture to leave it to the nation, and indeed to get rid of it to a good home as soon as ever possible. The wife points out that although her mamma is Italian, she has been over here with us a few months, and has got a travel pass, so this should assist in overcoming any rules and regs re exhibiting foreigners. Also the wife has just added that the mamma is quite distinguished in that she was Secretary President of the Rabbit Appreciation Society (Manzana branch) for about 12 years in the 1930s until it's abolition by Mussolini.

Could you send a courier round one morning to collect the masterpiece?
Many thanks

Yours sincerely
RM Morello (Mr)

R.M. Morello
Park View Road
Ealing
London W5

29 November 2005

Dear Mr Morello:

Thank you for your letter offering the gallery a portrait of your mother-in-law.

According to the collecting policy of the gallery, our collection should consist of people who have made a significant contribution to our national life so it is possible that this portrait may not meet our rules of eligibility.

In addition we must often apply such rules with some rigour since our collection is expanding steadily all the time and we may only have a limited amount of display space at any one time.

We are grateful, nonetheless, to you for thinking of our gallery and hope that you may have greater success in finding an appropriate home for your painting elsewhere.

Yours sincerely,

Tim Moreton

Dr Tim Moreton
Collections Manager

National Portrait Gallery St Martin's Place London WC2H 0HE
www.npg.org.uk

The General Manager
Debenham's Department Store
1 Welbeck Street
London W1E 0AA

Dear Sir or Madam

It is with deep regret that I must announce that the wife's mamma, Annunziata (aged 88), who's been kipping with us for a few weeks from Sicily, has let it be known that she will now be staying on in Ealing over the whole of Christmas and the New Year.

Quite apart from the shock that this unexpected news has engendered across the family, it also sets up a string of problems re accommodation. Just for starters when Ted and Doris Bostock arrive on Boxing Day from Eastbourne, can they both fit in the spare bedroom while the old bird is still clinging on there – or will someone be heading for the pigeon shed at the end of the back garden each night with a hot water bottle?

The reason for the old dear's bombshell is that she got hold of a which she's since been reading avidly. She is now requiring each of the family to buy her a "reward" (as she refers to Xmas presents) from Debenham's and reckons she's in with a chance if she holds on in the household till circa Dec 24th . To my horror she's homed in on the connoisseur's section, and in particular the *"Super de Luxe"* hamper – with a **price tag of £5,000!**

We hope you may accept some responsibility for the situation, which could turn tricky (Nb: the mother in law can be dodgy – even now no-one knows what became of her husband Federico after that trip to Beachy Head in 1962 when they had an unpleasant row about marmosets, and he was never seen again). We reckon that anything we can prove came from Debenham's might do. I've tried suggesting we buy her some **travel gear** , but she's not interested.

So here's a few items we'd like to order if you can confirm they're in stock:

- **nasal hair clippers**
- trampoline
- false teeth cleanser
- pipe and tobacco kit (the old trout's been smoking since about age 14).

I may have misheard but I'm sure I heard the old thing say she wants to *"dress up like a fairy"* on Xmas Day. Have you got any outsize kiddie's fancy dress that might accommodate a figure c 4 foot 11", long thin arms and hunchback?

Hoping to hear soon. All the best for the festive season,

Yours sincerely

RM Morello (Mr)

1 Welbeck Street
London W1G 0AA

www.debenhams.com

Mr R.M Morello
Park View Road
Ealing
London W5

155155/pc/unkwn

5th December 05

Dear Mr Morello

I acknowledge receipt of your letter dated 20th November and would like to thank you for considering us to be able to supply that special present for your loved ones.

May I suggest that your contact our Personal Shopper on 0207 518 7432, who will be more than happy to discuss your requirements, and is very experienced in making suggestions for that very special gift for relative's of all shapes and sizes.

I hope this has been of assistance to you and please accept Debenhams seasonal best wishes for you and your very unique family.

Yours sincerely

Paul Cavanagh
Senior Advisor
Customer Relations

Debenhams Retail plc. Registered in England. Company no. 83395. Registered office 1 Welbeck Street, London W1G 0AA.

Ian Addicoat Esq
President
Paranormal Research Organisation
PO Box 193
Penzance
Cornwall TR18 2ZT

Dear Mr Addicoat

I and the Mrs (Rosetta) are fascinated by the underworld of paranormals, and abnormal happenings. Having previously lived for many years in the countryside down the southwest we now miss these phenomenals. We are thinking of a return visit with Enoch and hope we might meet up, say on a ghost hunt.

Last Tuesday we were relaxing quite late one evening on the sofa. We both noticed some strange shapes on the ceiling, gently moving around. The lights were down and it was indistinct but the wife felt quite strongly there were vague goat shapes possibly. Unfortunately as she leapt up slowly she kicked over the bottle of crème de menthe and, the moment she shouted, all the figures dispersed and the shadows coalesced into a single large blob, or orb.

Is it possible we saw something we shouldn't've such as a paranormal? There could've been some gentle whistling at the same time, though the wife's mother is staying at present and tends to whistle a little while sleeping if she's left her dentures in, so we can't put this all down at this stage as a definite UFO etc.

I would very much like to join a paranormal organisation but feel the wife could be a liability as she's so noisy and excitable which could lead to the inhibition and upset of the ghosts.

Please forgive my English which is not that good anyway. Hoping to hear soon.

All the best

Yours sincerely

RM Morello (Mr).

9th of February 2006

Dear Mr Morello,

Thank you for your letters dated 21st of November & 29th of December.

I am sorry I did not reply sooner but because I get so many letters it just isn't unfortunately possible to reply quickly to them all.

If you wanted to apply to join P.R.O. then you would need to download a form from the website.

I have also included a leaflet about Ghost Nights for your interest. Hope that helps.

Kind regards

Ian Addicoat (President)

The Paranormal Research Organisation is a non-profit organisation dedicated to proficient study into the paranormal. We are considerate, experienced and above all consummately professional.

MORELLO'S MENAGERIES

Park View Road
Ealing
London W5
3 April 2006

Ian Addicoat Esq
President
Paranormal Research Organisation
PO Box 193
Penzance
Cornwall TR18 2ZT

Dear Mr Addicoat

The Mrs and I would like to thank you very much for your letter of 9th of February 2006 and for the leaflet re ghosts and for details of the website with stuff about forms etc which we've looked at and thought about a lot.

As a result we're even more interested in ghosts and paranormals than before. However the wife, whose the trousers of this operation although not that attractive (business end of rhino etc) states that I must raise some enquiries regarding the ghosts which we haven't spotted answers to in the leaflet.

Mainly it's to do with what happens if we were able to catch a ghost or other phenomenal. The Mrs believes there may have been a ghost in the back garden a few nights ago. She was just mucking out the marmosets. Suddenly there was a lot of rustling behind the rhododendron bush over by the meerkats' pen. They seemed very agitated and were standing in a circle, all staring at the bush as if it was quite suspicious. Several of the meerkats were chattering nervously and a couple of the gents at the front were hissing and showing off their bottoms at the bush even though their wives were trying to stop them. **Then there was a sudden vague groaning noise from the bush and all the 'kats rushed into their kennel. Also one of the cockatoos started screeching and it's crest shot up which only happens when it sees something suspicious (like a ghost).**

We don't know what the ghosts eat but the Mrs has since been leaving out a saucer of milk for them every night in the back garden. **Every morning it's been empty.** So now the wife's laid a little trap for the ghosts involving a net to do with her hairnets.

Mrs Morello enquires whether, if we trapped a ghost, it would be ok to place it in a cage with the emus as there's a bit of space there and they're probably about the same size so it should be better than with the kangaroos, which are slightly larger. And kick a lot.

Hoping to hear soon. What exactly do baby ghosts like to eat the wife has just enquired?

All the best

Yours sincerely

RM Morello (Mr)

122

PO BOX 193, PENZANCE, CORNWALL, TR18 2ZT
E-mail: info@paranormalresearch.org.uk

13th of April 2006

Dear Mr Morello,

Thank you for your letter dated 3rd of April 2006..

Also thanks for telling me about your activity.

As a Paranormal Researcher it is important not to jump to any conclusions about ghosts and supernatural activity, however for once I would have to say that it would certainly seem that something "very" strange is going on.

It must be very distressing to find your animals so affected and that your "Mrs" is having such a problem with a cockatoo!

As for what baby ghosts eat? It is not something I have studied in detail but perhaps I might suggest "Dreaded Wheat" or "Marley's rusks"!

I hope your problems are resolved and you reach a satisfactory conclusion.

With regards

END OF CORRESPONDENCE

Ian Addicoat

P.R.O. (UK)

Park View Road
Ealing
London W5

22 November 2005

British School of Taxidermy
Trefeglwys
Caersws
Powys SY17 5QQ

Dear Sirs

Re: Taxidermy

I have received a recommendation on your skills from some old friends in Caersws. I believe you may be the only taxidermists in the village.

We have two charming little dachshunds, Fritz and Adolf. Both have wobbly rear legs, and Adolf can no longer chew his biscuits; nor does he enjoy chasing pigeons any more. Sadly the hounds' days could well be numbered.

What would you estimate as the cost of a complete taxidermal stuffing of the two, and a nice mounting in a good quality glass case with a diorama round them with a bone, dog bed, and a couple of pigeons to set it off?

We expect to be visiting some old friends, the Bamfords (Betty and Stan), in Cardiff over Christmas and could bring along the hounds to see you then. Can you inspect the object before its decease to measure up etc and give a quote, then hold the price for a while?

I should be most grateful to hear soon.

Many thanks for your help,

Yours sincerely

Rosetta Morello (Mrs)

THE BRITISH SCHOOL OF TAXIDERMY
NEUADD DDU, LLANGURIG, LLANIDLOES SY18 6RX

27th November 2005

Dear Mrs Morello,

Thank you for your enquiry about Fritz and Adolf. This must be a very difficult time for you all and there is no need to make it any more heartrending by visiting the taxidermist over Christmas!

Mark can do all that is necessary when the time comes, as long as you make arrangements for them both to be deep frozen within 24 hours. Most vets will usually help with this service for you and there is an (optional) local pets crematorium here, if you wish, for after the taxidermy.

As a rough estimate, the work you describe will cost around £2,000, with the pigeons supplied by us. Any adjustments to the price take place after Mark has seen Fritz and Adolf (re condition, etc.) and you then make your decision to proceed by payment of 50% deposit.

A much-loved Dalmation is taking up his time at the moment, so we shall be able to show you photos of that, once completed. Meanwhile, do visit www.theonlytaxidermist.com for references about his gifted work over the past 25 years.

Yours sincerely,

Sally

Sally Winston-Smith

PS. Please note change of address above ... we moved from Trefeglwys last year but still have a Royal Mail re-direction order!

Morello's Cakes and Fancies

park View Road
Ealing
London W5

26 November 2005

Fern Britton and Philip Scofield
"This Morning"
BBC TV
Wood Lane
White City
London W12

Dear Fern and Philip

The whole family love your show, so much that the kids bunk off school, and also we've rigged up a tiny tv to the bakery round the back so Sammy and me and Rochelle can watch it while Sammy sorts out his nuts and we do the flans for lunch.

Unfortunately the wife's mum Annunziata (whose knocking on 89) is kipping with us at present (from Manzana, Sicily). Even more unfortunately she got hold of the TV remote on Thursday, and saw the piece on nipple piercing. Since then our second (Amphora, 14) has been showing her mags etc on the subject.

Now the ma-in-law is determined what she wants for Xmas – a complete once over including nipple clamps and *"gimps"*, and something called a **Butt-Lifter**, plus a chain from nostril to ear then up to the eyebrow possibly. And something else I can't mention in this lettre.

Amphora's egging her on , and reckons the old bird can join her girl's gang (the "Park View Hood") if she gets the gear.

Could you put us in touch v urgently with the Doc who was on your show talking about nipples etc. With any luck he can head her off from a disaster, and explain that while it makes good sense for a youngster to get clamps and metals hanging off you everywhere it could be dodgy etc for an old buzzard what with the antipathetic etc you need in the operation to knock you out etc.

We would be so relieved for an early response.

Is Fern getting any clamping done? The wife reckons she read Phil's already got one gizmo possibly.

Many thank yous
Yours sincerely

RM Morello (Mr)

NO REPLY

126

Park View Road
Ealing
London W5

3 December 2005

~~Mark Austin Esq.~~ Jon Snow Esq
~~News at Ten~~ Channel 4 News
ITV
London TV Centre
Upper Ground
London SE1 9LT

Dear Mr Austin

We all think you're a great newscaster – especially the ladies in the family.

So does our neighbour Mrs Singanayaragaram, who is an elderly lady living alone with a parrot and a couple of canaries. Mrs S was born in a different age and background from loads of folks we know. Consequentially she finds electrical implements rather confusing. She only first saw a telly when she arrived in the UK from Ceylon in 1990 (approx).

For quite a long time Mrs Singanayaragaram got TV sets muddled up with microwaves - with some unfortunate results. Consequentially hours have gone by as she's tried tuning in her Zanussi P450 microwave to her favourite programme, *Bullseye* with Jim Bowen. Likewise you yourself when reading the news on *News at Ten* have often received an unwelcome plate of Tesco Finest Cumberland Pie right in the cakehole when least expecting it. I can only apologise for this from Mrs S.

The present electrical problem is that the old dear, who loves the telly, refuses to turn on the set in her bedroom as she's become convinced that any stars looking out from the telly can see her undressing in the evening. So in order to view *Emmerdale Farm* at bedtime she's taken to undressing in the sitting room – behind a screen.

The situation is still causing Mrs S (aged 72, approx) some anxiety. Would you be agreeable to setting the good lady's mind at rest by writing a small note confirming that it is <u>not</u> possible for you to see Mrs Singanayaragaram in her nightie (or the altogether possibly) through the screen when reading the news? It seems that only when she sees this in print that will she accept this is the case.

Your help would be very much appreciated.

With best wishes and many thanks
Yours sincerely

RM Morello (Mr)

200 Gray's Inn Road
London WC1X 8XZ

23rd December 2005

R M Morello
    Park View Road
Ealing
London W5

Dear Mr Morello

I fear you are confused. I have to tell you that I have been consuming Tesco's Cumberland Pie thanks to Mrs S over a considerable period of time.

My idea is that I had no idea it came from her. Furthermore, 72 years old she may be but even if through a screen I would like to assure her she is in the most remarkable condition. This is a lady who has taken very good care of herself even if the trials of modern technology have alluded her. Please assure her that all her secrets are safe with me.

Further, may I take this opportunity to wish you and all the ladies in your family a particularly warm and nutritious Christmas and a special word of affection for Mrs S.

Best regards.

Jon Snow
Channel 4 News

END OF CORRESPONDENCE

Registered Office 200 Gray's Inn Road London WC1X 8XZ Registered Number 548648 England
Independent Television News Limited

park View Road
Ealing
London W5

29 December 2005

Dr William Foster
Department of Zoology
University of Cambridge
Downing Street
Cambridge CB2 3EJ

Dear Dr Foster

I have been referred to you as a leading authority on spiders. I would be most grateful for some guidance.

The other night when the kids were out, the wife and I were watching a programme by David Attenborough. There were two spiders who were courting, with a view I believe to starting a family. It was rather a pleasant prospect after the strains and stresses of the Christmas preparations that have told on both me and the Mrs.

The gentleman spider was a small and rather meek creature, who conducted himself thoughtfully, and with creditable dignity. He was pleasant and easy in his manner, as far as one could tell. The female in contrast was large, menacing and vexatious, and made several unsettling lurching movements towards the gent.

During the programme I caught Mrs Morello (Rosetta) glancing at me several times through her large spectacles, and looking away quickly just as I caught her eye. After a while she hauled her huge frame out of the armchair, rose to her feet and headed ponderously for the kitchen, to make a toasted sandwich she said.

At this point Sir David cut in, explaining in hushed tones that immediately the spiders had mated, the female – without a word of thanks or even an explanation – set upon her husband and ate him, including all the legs.

Mrs Morello returned slowly from the kitchen. I noticed her very slightly chuckling under her breath. She said she had decided not to make a sandwich after all, as she had *"thought of something else"*. A little while later the Mrs asked if I felt like an early night. I declined.

The rest of the evening was spent in icy silence, watching *Strictly Come Dancing*.

Do you have any information on spiders you could provide, first class? Are humans in any way related to spiders?

Please reply to me, not the wife.
Yours respectfully

RM Morello (Mr)

Z *Department of*
oology

Downing Street
Cambridge CB2 3EJ

William Foster PhD
Deputy Head of Department (Teaching)

Web: www.zoo.cam.ac.uk

Mr R.M.Morello
Park View Road
Ealing
London W5

January 4th 2006

Dear Mr Morello

Thank you for your intriguing letter of the 29th inst. Spiders are not really my field, but I am interested in Sexual Selection, whose iron laws apply to all sexually reproducing animals, including yourself and Mrs Morello. We probably share about 75% (this is a guess only) of our genes with spiders, but this is probably not specially relevant since we share 50% of our genes with the banana. [You should perhaps not share this intelligence with Mrs Morello, since she might be tempted to experiment with one of your appendages to spice up her smoothies].

Female spiders do not usually gain much food value from eating their mates, who are in any case much smaller than they are. It is simply that they are very strongly programmed to eat anything that comes on to their web. The male is just a snack really: but he will normally be under strong selection to avoid being eaten. One possible exception to this is the Red Back Spider of Australia. Here (it is thought) the male actually *gains* by being eaten, since this stops the female from mating again for quite a long period. That way, the male (even though now dead) might ensure that his genes (rather than a rival's) get into the next generation. I suppose a similar scenario might apply to you and your wife, but only if you were both still playing the field.

As it happens, Mrs Foster (Angela) and I both watched the *Silk-Makers* programme (note the feeble, timid avoidance of the word *Spiders* in the title). She also started to get a little excited as she watched the plump females draining the bodily fluids from their mates. But I know that her chief passion is alcohol, not nourishment, so I am probably not at much risk [though I suppose she might attempt to ferment a liqueur from my rotting corpse, but this seems like a long game]. Just to be on the safe side, I prepared her her favourite tipple of Bombay Sapphire Gin and Tonic: she dosed off presently, so the period of danger was avoided, and I was able to watch *Pop Idol* in peace.

I hope this helps a little
Yours truly

130

MORELLO'S MENAGERIES

park View Road
Ealing
London W5

29 December 2005

The Sales Director
Ensign Bus Co
Juliette Close
Purfleet Industrial Park
Purfleet
Essex RM15 4YF

Dear Sir

The wife and I were rather shocked to read that you're flogging off all the red Routemaster buses still knocking around London in favour of some bendy serpentine things that snake silently about the streets. Still, the world's got to move on.

Me and the Mrs (Rosetta) did our courting on the back seat at the top of the old number 97 that wound around Ealing, and the no. 65 that chugged up from Chessington and through Richmond to Ealing Broadway. We used to scoff two bags of chips and a haddock and plaice with a gherkin some Saturday nights on the way back from the Acton Empire after watching Spartacus or Ben Hur.

Can I buy one of the buses, maybe one of the ones we rode on? We want to re-enact *"Summer Holiday"*, where Sir Cliff Richard dressed up as a Beach Boy, with Una Stubbs and that peachy bloke off *"It Ain't Alf Ot Mum"*. Afterwards we thought to parking it down the end of the back garden near the old pigeon shed as it might make a nice home for some of the larger birds including the ostrich and the kangaroos we got in recently.

Mrs Morello loves the bigger animals and wants a bit more luxury for them. She especially likes the flightless birds who peck around the place and shove their heads in the sandpit.

The wife reckons she'd stop a bullet for that emu.

The Mrs also likes *"On the Buses"* with Reg Varney and Blakey, so we might do that too. In fact she's a bit of a ringer for Olive (tho somewhat less glamorous in my view).

What's the damage on one of the old bangers please? Could we get a refund if it turns out to be a crate or we don't need the engine anyway due to the birdhouse plan?

Also do you have any in pink the wife has just enquired?

Many thanks for your help and look forward to hearing soon.
Yours sincerely

RM Morello (Mr)

Ensignbus

www.ensignbus.com

Mr. R. M. Morello,
Morello's Menageries,
   Park View Road,
Ealing,
London,
W5

Juliette Close
Purfleet Industrial Park
Purfleet
Essex RM15 4YF

sales@ensignbus.com

5th January 2006

Dear Mr. Morello,

Thank you for your letter of 29th December 2005 and your enquiry about purchasing a Routemaster bus.

However, we have now sold all of the Routemaster buses we previously had for sale so we cannot help you on this occasion.

Yours sincerely,

P.P. Steve Newman
DIRECTOR

END OF CORRESPONDENCE

Registered Office: Ensign Bus Company Ltd, Juliette Way, Purfleet Industrial Park, London Road, South Ockendon, Essex RM15 4YA
Registered in England & Wales Number 2656574

Park View Road
Ealing
London W5
31 December 2005

Dr Alex Morton
AR Morton & Associates
Dental Surgeons
20 Haven Green
Ealing
London W5 2UP

Dear Doc

An unfortunate and harrowing incident took place over the Xmas hols. which calls for your expert attention.

The mother-in-law, Annunziata, (pushing 89) has been kipping with us for a few weeks, with little sign of heading back to her shack in Sicily or otherwise moving on. On Boxing Day afternoon we had an unexpected visit from the local estate agent , Dudley Grocock, and his partner, Doreen, who are our new neighbours. They brought half a bottle of tia maria and some cheese biscuits. Clearly Dudley was trying to make amends after Mrs Morello had placed some form of spell or fatwa on them after Dudley was seen knocking an unauthorised For Sale sign into the rosebed in our front garden the previous Tuesday morning.

After tea Dudley, who was showing off his new digital camera to the family, pointed the device at the wife's ma and - without warning or provocation ....asked her to smile.

At once everything stopped. Tosti ceased picking his spots, his crooked finger in mid air. Amphora looked in horror over the top of her specs. Rizzo dropped the train he'd been winding up. The budgies huddled up together in their cage. Even the wife's knitting needles stopped clattering. A horrible silence enveloped the room. Somewhere in the distance a rook crowed harshly. Just a clock ticking on the mantelpiece.

Slowly, with a creak, the granmamma's mouth began to widen. The hideous face opened up, the lips spread apart and, just as the flash went off....the old buzzard's dentures fell out into her lap. No one has seen such a horrible sight in years as then presented itself with this ghastly vacant face crowned with a horrible gaping mouth and lolling tongue. Doreen started screaming and had to be dragged out of the room while Amphora seemed vaguely to faint.

We tried everything to get the teeth back in, and finally managed to wedge them in with a mixture of Polyfilla and Bostik. During the process Dudley received quite a nasty bite and had to leave hurriedly.

Can we get the old trout round to you quite rapidly for some damage limitation and aesthetic treatment, with or without anaesthetics? Please just give the word.

Yours in anxious anticipation,

RM Morello (Mr)

DR. A.R. MORTON & ASSOCIATES.
DENTAL SURGEONS

The Haven Green Clinic
20/23 Haven Green
Ealing, London W5 2UP

10 January 2006

Mr R M Morello
    Park View road
Ealing
London
W5

Dear Mr Morello,

Happy New Year to your and your family.

I was so sorry to read your harrowing account of poor Annunziata's dental disaster over the Christmas period. Boxing Day does seem to have a bad reputation over recent years, and I hope the emotional Tsunami you all suffered is beginning to subside.

Your Sicilian mother-in-law should indeed be seen urgently to test her for the toxic affects of your Bostik/Polyfilla remedy. I am sure with modern dental technology we shall be able to offer Annunziata a solution to her embarrassing and distressing dental woes. Incidentally the human bite suffered by Dudley Grocock should also be thoroughly investigated as there is a high infection rate after this form of trauma.

We can discuss the best form of anxiety management and pain control for Annunziata at her consultation visit. If you would like us to use minimal anaesthetic during her treatment I am sure we could work towards that.

Yours sincerely,

DR ALEX A MORTON
B.D.S. (London) M.F.D.S.
R.C.S. (Eng) M.F.G.D.P (UK)
DIP. D. Sed (Guys)
M.Sc. Implant Dentistry (London)

AAM/cal

Park View Road
Ealing
London W5

1 jan. 2006 !

Richard Baker
Chief Executive
Boots Opticians
1 Thane Road
Nottingham NG90 1BS

Dear Mr Baker

May I wish you and all your staff and customers a very happy and prosperous New Year. All our family think Boots is brilliant esp. over Christmas. We love your food esp the wife, though she prefers to avoid the dietary produce as low calories tend to interfere with her metrabolistics.

In fact the Mrs (Rosetta) had a bit of an incident over Xmas with her opticals. **She was struggling into the dining room laden with a massive turkey when her spectaculars got all steamed up. So she chucked them on her seat whilst parking the beast. 2 mins later she returned with the brussels, sat down and ....kerrunch! End of goggles.**

So now the Mrs needs a new pair of Gregorys innit?

I was going to write to Ian Filby, your head of Beauty and Lifesytle, but as all this concerns the wife (goggle-eyed monster of the deep etc) I thought it may not be appropriate probably.

Could you do a pretty heavy pair with industrial use in mind as Mrs M likes to get stuck into hefty duties such as the mucking out, and breaking rocks whilst gardening?

Also, do you do little opticles for the animals? We have a parrot, Russell, which is constantly twisting his head around then looking upwards for hours at a blank ceiling, which must be quite boring. Possibly a tiny pair with a string like old dames have in case they drop off into something unpleasant on the floor of the cage.

Look forward to hearing soon.

Happy New year etc.

Yours sincerely

RM Morello (Mr)

CE\2997809
12 January 2006

Boots Group Plc
Richard Baker
Chief Executive
D94 Building
Nottingham
NG90 1BS

Mr R M Morello
 Park View Road
Ealing
LONDON W5

Dear Mr Morello

Thanks for your letter addressed to Richard. I'm replying on behalf of Richard, who is out and about on business within our stores.

May I wish you and your family a Happy New Year too. What a pleasure it was to receive your complimentary letter.

However, I'm sorry to learn of the mishap with the wife's glasses when they met with her derrière and were squashed. A hefty bird, by the sound of things, the turkey, of course, not Mrs M.

We'd be pleased to help her out with a replacement pair. Our Optics in Ealing, New Broadway has great offers and promotions during January, I'm sure we could fix her up with a pair suitable for all domesticate. Their telephone number is 0208 567 5326 if she'd like to make an appointment.

As for optics for the animals, I'm enclosing some goggles, as a special treat for Russell. We've made them especially for him. We hope it relieves the boredom of ogling the blank ceiling. If this doesn't work, I can only suggest painting a pretty Polly, on it - surely that'd do the trick!.

Again, all the best to you Sir, and your family.

Best wishes,

Lorraine Scott

Lorraine Scott
Customer Manager
Chief Executive's Office

END OF CORRESPONDENCE

Boots Group PLC
Registered in England & Wales
4452715
Registered office
1 Thane Road West
Nottingham NG2 3AA

www.boots.com

Park View Road
Ealing
London W5

1 January 2006

The Managing Director
DVLA
Longview Road
Swansea SA6 7JL

Dear Sir

I must relate an unfortunate and harrowing incident that occurred over the Xmas hols on (and off) the public highway which demands your intervention.

Whilst storming down The Avenue, W5 in our Fiat 600 (pale blue with rust) the Mrs swerved violently and lost control of the beast, nudging Morrie Needleman and his Ford Prefect into the front window of *Daphne's Florists*. Wrestling with the wheel, the wife careered across the road, bashing into Jose and Juanita's greengrocers' shop, *The Little Pea*, and coming to rest by *Lucky Joe's* - the adult entertainment shop.

In fact a large letter "P" fell onto the roof of the Fiat from *Lucky Joe's*, which now proclaims itself to be THE BEST MEN'S ORN SHOP IN EALING.

Mrs Morello states that the reason for her loss of control was seeing a driver approach who was horrendously ugly. It was a gent with a massive bulbous nose, a large red thick ear and two huge buck teeth. On top of all this the monster seemed to be making a gargoyle type face at the wife as they passed. She was unable to get his number but saw him race away in what showed every sign of being an Austin Allegro.

Is there not a case for banning drivers whose ugly appearance is just so hideous it might be objectively considered to pose a threat or at least a nuisance to other road users, especially if they've only got clapped out motors anyway? Maybe every roaduser should have to present to a traffic warden for a visual MOT when applying to renew their licence or their tax disc?

Please advise whether this useful expedient can be shoved in one of your leaflets as soon as possible. Exceptions could be made for certain celebrities and politicians who, though hideous, have essential need of a motor to get to gigs etc. I am raising this matter with my local MP who may well be in agreement.

Last time I wrote in I didn't hear for about six months so just hoping for a reply before I'm wishing you happy New Year 2007 ! - the tax disc comes up this month.

Yours sincerely

RM Morello (Mr)

Cc: Stephen Pound Esq MP (Ealing North)
    Barry Manilow

Driver and Vehicle Licensing Agency
Director External and Corporate Services
C3 West/Zone 4
DVLA
Longview Road
Swansea
SA6 7JL

R M Morello Esq
    Park View Road
Ealing
LONDON W5

Website   www.direct.gov.uk/motoring

Your Ref
Our Ref

Date: 6 January 2006

Dear Mr Morello

Thank you for your letter of 1 January – one of the most amusing we have received for some time.

I very much hope that Mrs Morello received no serious injury as a result of the accident you describe.

Drivers have to cope with many distractions. It would be quite impossible and impractical to legislate to remove them all particularly where they are as subjective as the case you mention.

I hope that encouraged by this rapid response you will be able to get round to taxing your car in good time!

Yours sincerely

Trevor Horton
Director External and Corporate Services
C3 West/Zone 4

CUSTOMER SERVICE EXCELLENCE   INVESTOR IN PEOPLE

An executive agency of the
Department for
Transport

Park View Road
Ealing
London W5

1 January 2006

Mr Stephen Pound MP
House of Commons
Westminster
London SW1A 1AA

Dear Mr Pound

I understand you are my MP, and that I voted for you. Happy New Year (unless you are Liberal Democrat).

I attach a letter I wrote to the senior honcho at the DVLA which carries some pertinent views with which you may be in agreement, and possibly find yourself in sympathy with given the circumstances adumbrated therein.

If you have the chance to get down to the Palace of W some time in the coming year and feel like stretching the hind legs, may I suggest this might be a good cause to get your teeth into.

 It could be argued that the underlying idea if badly handled in drafting the legislation could tend to undermine civil liberties, so you should have plenty of Front Bench support immediately.

Yours sincerely

RM Morello (Mr)

To: A.M. Novello.

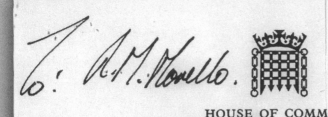

HOUSE OF COMMONS
LONDON SW1A 0AA

26th January 06

Dear Mr Novello,

Many thanks for your letter of the 1st January.

You make an entirely reasonable point and I will endeavour to raise the matter in the House.

With best wishes,

[signature]

Park View Road
Ealing
London W5

2 January 2006

M. Roux
Le Gavroche
43 Upper Brook Street
London W1K 7QR

Dear M. Roux

Mrs Morello and I think that your restaurant is a quite marvellous establishment, and we believe leads the way as far as molecular gastronomy is concerned. We love your progressive menu, with superb confections in lovely surroundings innit.

The wife wishes to apply for a job with you, as sous chef. Her specialism is rustic artisanal Sicilian dishes (her folks come from Manzana). This cuisine is characterised by simple wholesome country ingredients available at any country market stall or from under a tree etc. or beside a road. She's already knocked up a few confections for the local WI. Amongst the more popular have been:

Bisque du souris curieuse; petit assortement de dormouse; ballotine of guinea pig with pipistrelle sauce and a hint of compost; delice of pan-fried stoat in fennel with peach mousse; rabbit surprise sautee with braised baby kangaroo slices aux prunes lightly tossed in Cadbury's fruit and nut avec lobster supreme; fricasee of ferret with tournedos of poached yak in a light gerbil coulis. Helium cocoa.

Hoping to hear soon. Apologies that we're Italian.

With kind regards

Respectfully yours

RM Morello (Mr)

Le Gavroche Ltd.

43 Upper Brook Street, London W1K 7QR

Email: bookings@le-gavroche.com / Website: www.le gavroche.co.uk / www.michelroux.co.uk

8 January 2006

Mr. R.M. Morello
Park View Road
Ealing
London W5

Dear Mr. Morello,

Thank you for your kind and humorous letter, I am glad to hear that you enjoy Le Gavroche but do take issue with your remark about molecular gastronomy. You surely have mistaken me for my friend and colleague Heston Blumenthal.

As for your wife, I regret that I have no positions available at present or even in the foreseeable future.

Thank you also for the inspirational menu that could get you in trouble with the RSPCA so please be careful.

Kind regards,

Michel Roux

RELAIS &
CHATEAUX.

Managing Director: Michel Albert Roux - Directors: Albert Roux & Silvano Giraldin - Chairman: Lord Sharman of Redlynch
Registered Office 43 Upper Brook Street, London W1K 7QR   Registered No. 1825199 England

Park View Road
Ealing
London W5

2January 2006

Gordon Ramsay Esq
Restaurant Gordon Ramsay
68 Royal Hospital Road
London SW3 4HP

Dear Mr Ramsay

Mr Morello and I think that your restaurant is a quite marvellous establishment, and we believe leads the way as far as molecular gastronomy is concerned. We love your progressive menu, with superb confections in lovely surroundings.

We wish to offer up our son Tosti (17) for a job with you, as sous chef. His specialism is rustic artisanal Sicilian dishes (our folks come from Manzana). This cuisine is characterised by simple wholesome rural ingredients available at any country market stall or from under a tree etc. or beside a road. He's already knocked up a few confections for the local WI. Amongst the more popular have been:

Bisque du souris curieuse; petit assortement de dormouse; ballotine of guinea pig with pipistrelle sauce and a hint of compost; delice of pan-fried stoat in fennel with peach mousse; rabbit surprise sautee with braised baby kangaroo slices aux prunes lightly tossed in Cadbury's fruit and nut avec lobster supreme; fricasee of ferret with tournedos of poached yak in a light gerbil coulis. Helium cocoa.

We believe Tosti will be ideal for you. He likes to move slowly about the place and will benefit from a patient, low pressure environment where tolerance, patience and understanding are the key words. He is unpunctual, and is given to moods and fantasy-thinking. He likes to paint his nails, recite poetry and strum romantic ballads on the guitar throughout the day. He's done 3 months at the Constance Spry School of Etiquette but found it rather stressful.

Hoping to hear soon. Apologies that we're Italian.

Yours sincerely

Rosetta Morello (Mrs)

Mrs Rosetta Morello
Park View Road
Ealing
London W5

16th January 2006

Dear Mrs Morello,

Please accept our compliments to both yourself and Mr Morello and we thank you for your kind remarks regarding Royal Hospital Road.

Most interesting to hear about your son, Tosti (17) He sounds just the sort of talent that we are forever striving to recognise and set apart. Viewing the list of confections that Tosti has prepared it immediately comes to mind that he would be very useful to us in our new project which involves a field kitchen in one of the World's war zones. It is in these theatres of conflict that people's minds turn to thoughts of comfort food and this is so obviously a speciality of Tosti.

The outline that you have described concerning Tosti's kitchen modus operandi is pretty well ideal for de-stressing soldiers fresh in from a long day on the battlefield and I cannot thank you enough for the suggestion.

Whilst we cannot guarantee immediate employment we are taking the opportunity to enclose a job application for Tosti and if he feels able to complete it during the coming months somewhere or other, we can further consider a job for him.

With kind regards,

Chris Hutcheson
CEO
Gordon Ramsay Holdings

Enc.

GORDON RAMSAY HOLDINGS LIMITED

1 CATHERINE PLACE
LONDON SW1E 6D

REGISTERED NO. 345720
ENGLAND

park View Road
Ealing
London W5

6 January 2006

The Managing Director
Townends Estate Agents
Head Office
Latour House
Chertsey Boulevard
Chertsey
Surrey KT16 9JX

Dear Sir

I must relate a serious incident which has occurred in your Ealing estate agency branch.

Mrs Morello (Rosetta) was round the branch last Tuesday riffling through some sales particulars for some quite posh mansion type properties, and enjoying a cup of coffee and the company of your staff while it was spitting a bit outside. Anyway she had some time to kill before meeting Hilda Champkin at the vet's.

The wife felt she recognised the gent sitting at the desk in the corner, being served by the lady with blonde hair in a beehive arrangement, and a large pendant down the décolletage. The gent had a wife or similar with him, and a tiny dog with bulging eyes. The creature seemed distinctly nervous, constantly looking around, and the gent kept feeding it choc drops.

Anyway the wife was rather preoccupied as she was also doing some knitting. But when she got home later she suddenly leapt up from her armchair whilst watching Emmerdale Farm, yelling that the gent she had seen was Saddam Hussein, probably. She said he had a suit on and a shirt. I asked if he had a tache, which she confirmed, which could well settle it.

Please alert your branch so they can check this out as I think Mr Hussein needs apprehending if he's escaped. He was after a small country cottage with wisteria round the front, and **no chain.** Around £250,000, but could go up to £300,000 for the right property in a nice area with planning permission for a large hole in the ground.

Many thanks for your help and look forward to hearing soon.

Yours sincerely

RM Morello (Mr)

13th January 2006

Park View Road
Ealing
London, W5

LATOUR HOUSE
CHERTSEY BOULEVARD
HANWORTH LANE
CHERTSEY KT16 9JX

group@townends.co.uk
townends.co.uk

Dear Mr Morello,

I have been handed your letter of 6th January, as Compliance Manager for the Group.

Thank you for informing us of your concerns with which we will deal.

Yours sincerely,

Mrs Cheryl Ram (LLB Hons)

Compliance Manager

Townends Group of over 40 offices
offer the following services

- Residential Sales
- Residential Lettings
- Financial Services
- Land & New Homes
- Surveying & Valuation
- Property Management
- Commercial
- Residential Investment
- Business Transfer
- Overseas
- Conveyancing Services

Townends Group Limited
Registered in England Number 3090178
Registered Office: Latour House, Chertsey Boulevard
Hanworth Lane, Chertsey, KT16 9JX
VAT 720 6373 15

The Townends Group includes:
Townends Estate Agents, Regents Estate Agents, Tyser Greenwood
Estate Agents , dnt Financial Services, dnt Investment Concepts,
Tyser Greenwood Surveyors

MORELLO'S MENAGERIES

park View Road
Ealing
London W5

6 January 2006

The Managing Director
Egg Banking PLC
1 Waterhouse Square
London EC1N 2NA

Dear Sir

The wife and me and the kids were very upset to see your ad in the press recently depicting a guinea pig or similar rodent-creature dressed up to the nines and advertising one of your financial products, viz an Egg card.

Whilst we like your products and also eat eggs regularly, we all felt the rodent looked very unhappy and put upon. It was being forced to stand on its hind legs, probably for several hours, without members of its family present, and with the strong implication in the ad that g-pigs are poor dressers, and fat and ugly to boot!

But the clothes were just too small, with tight troos, a pair of ill fitting pyjama tops buttoned up crooked with tum sticking out, and with scruffy boots flapping everywhere.

The whole assemblage looks absurd. Apart from everything the colours were all wrong.

Surely this is no way to treat an intelligent and sensitive creature in the 20th century?

If you're going to do up a rodent such as this, you need to measure them up, provide sneakers, levis and leather jacket, and a tiny comb so he/it can keep its cranial hair in shape, preferably in a quiff.

How can you expect the public to trust you to run a bank if you can't get the basics right?

Please confirm you let the little fellow go out the door after the snapshots, and haven't bounced him into some ridiculous fast track management course like that fat little bloke on the Halifax ads.

Yours sincerely

RM Morello (Mr)

Morello's Menageries
Park View Road
Ealing
London W5

3 February, 2006

Dear Mr Morello,

Thank you for your recent letter concerning our new Egg Card campaign.

Egg has a tradition of creating 'edgy' adverts and our guinea pigs campaign is no different. The guinea pigs have helped us provide a tongue-in-cheek metaphor of human behaviour and attitudes with reference to how people look at their finances. All images of the guinea pigs are mocked-up and I'd like to assure you and your family that at no point were any animals harmed in the making of the adverts.

You also expressed concern that the guinea pigs may have been put into a fast track management course within Egg or Halifax and I'd like to take this opportunity to assure you that this is not the case.

Thank you for your interest in our campaign.

Daniel Sector
Egg Banking plc

Egg is a trading name of the Egg group of companies which includes: Egg plc (reg. no. 2446340), Egg Banking plc (reg. no. 2999842) and Egg Financial Intermediation Ltd (reg. no. 3626259) which are both members of the General Insurance Standards Council, Egg Investments Ltd (reg. no. 3403963) which is regulated by the Financial Services Authority, Egg Financial Products Ltd (reg. no. 3319027), and Egg International Ltd (reg. no. 4059226). These members of the Egg group are registered in England and Wales. Registered offices: 1 Waterhouse Square, 138–142 Holborn, London EC1N 2NA.

Park View Road
Ealing
London W5
27 February 2006

Clive Aslet Esq
Editor in Chief
Country Life
King's Reach Tower
Stamford Street
London SE1 9LS

Dear Mr Aslet

The wife recently had an unfortunate experience with a toothpick. This occasioned her rapid conveyance in a supine posture in the BSA Bantam side car to the rooms of Mr Fenton Cheeseman, dental surgeon, in Bolsover Street.

At the time of our arrival an oriental gent was undergoing a very audible extraction of some odiferous effluvia from a tooth or teeth, which evidently entailed significant pain (two thirty). The procedure being well underway gave the opportunity for a thorough perusal of the waiting room and its contents. The Mrs' eye fell on some well thumbed issues of *Country Life* magazine, especially the section tucked in just before halfway, after the massive mansions for sale and before the ads section. This bit always shows various young ladies in ball gowns cuddling dogs and other farmyard animals but mostly advertising to find a hubbie, or possibly that they've just got one (what's that page called, by the by?).

The Mrs, although physically compromised, was able to stuff a couple of back numbers in her handbag - just moments before Mr Choo was wheeled out motionless on a trolley. She has since read these thoroughly back home. As a consequence she would like to advertise our second child in this slot, beneath a nice A5 snapshot, as follows:

Miss Amphora Morello

Amphora, who is 15 and a half and a little overweight, is the only daughter of Mr and Mrs RM Morello of Ealing, West London. Educated at St Marjorie's Girls' High, she is hoping to retake her GCSE's at the Percy Grainger Crammer asap. She hopes thereafter to pursue a career as a barmaid in Ealing Broadway somewhere.

Amphora is shown with her little ferret Stacie beside the pigeon shed in the back garden. She has recently split up after a brief liaison with Wayne, who is unlikely to return owing to the terms of his Asbo.

The Mrs (Rosetta) asks if you could very kindly provide your terms for this ad please in time for the lass's 16th in about three weeks time?

Many thanks for your courteous assistance

Yours sincerely

RM Morello (Mr)

149

Park View Road
Ealing
London W5

Matthew Hall Esq
Professional Hypnotist
50 Marlborough Road
Hillingdon
Uxbridge UB10 OP3

Dear Mr Hall

I was present when you hypnotated some geezer a couple of weeks back at the Ealing
Golf Club.   I was playing a handicap round with Mavis Niblock and Melvin Gaylord.
I whacked my ball off the 7th tee. Unfortunately it bounced off Ken Froggatt's
testimonials and then rolled up to the clubhouse.

I looked in through the window and saw you incantating to some elderly gent sitting
opposite who seemed fast asleep. It all seemed a bit spooky. Anyway a bit later I
came over all funny, and found myself standing at the bar with my trousers over my
head and my specs all steamed up.

Is this all part of the service?

Yours sincerely

RM Morello

RM Morello (Mr)

PS: the wife prefers me like this as she reckons it brings a bit of mystery back into the
conjugals.

PPS: did the other bloke go nuts?

Matthew Hall, DCH, DHP

The Optimum Health Clinic,
106, Gordon Rd,
Ealing W13

Dear Mr. Morello,
 I was very sorry to hear of your assault at Ealing Golf Club. It must have
been excruciatingly painful to have your ball whacked all that way. You do
seem to have suffered hallucinations, and whether the trousers over your
head were real or not, I think you have a genuine case to sue your
opponent. I happen to know of a brilliant lawyer, who is very good at
dealing with these cases. I would be very happy to make a referral to him -
just give me the nod.
 However, your wife seems very happy with the current situation, so you
may not want to bother. If an accidental spot of Sado Masachism has
boosted your sex life I could also refer you to the BDSM website(I , of
course, have only visited it for research purposes). Sand M is very popular.
But if you or your wife need help with spicing up your love life, then
hypnosis can help there too.
    With best wishes,

        Matthew Hall

151

MORELLO'S MENAGERIES

Park View Road
Ealing
London W5

13 March 2006

Dr Lord George Carey
The House of Lords
Westminster
London SW1

Dear Lord Carey

Mrs Morello has been very upset at Eric's Electricals, the contractors we used last winter to restore the heating to the parrot and pigeon sheds. Wires and strings etc mean diddly squat to me and we thought they might be quite good. But no sooner had they left than everything went whizz bang crash, and the end of the shack blew off into the fishpond. The macaws kept screaming for about 3 days!

The wife's also convinced that her unusual scorpion brooch (which she has **always** worn to chair Bowls Club committee meetings) was missing after Eric's men had withdrawn.

I recently read of you that:

"**George Carey was once a clerk at the Electricity Board and became Archbishop of Canterbury in 1991. He led the Church of England and 80 million Anglicans around the world.**"

I appreciate it was quite a few years back but I wonder if you are in touch with any sparkies you can recommend? They must be **reliable** and **honest,** and have some **experience of animals.**

It's just so difficult to find a good workman in this day and ages. We just thought maybe you might be able to do the work, possibly? We could discuss terms if this would be of interest.

Hoping we might be able to hear soon and apologies that we're Italian etc.

Yours sincerely

RM Morello (Mr)

26. IV. 06

Dear Mr Morello

Thank you very much for your letter of March 13ᵗʰ. Please forgive the long delay in replying but I have been away a great deal and my correspondence has failed as a result.

I am sorry but I cannot help you with your Inquiry! There must be a hint of a joke in your question because I left the London Electricity Board 50 years ago! However, I can assure you that there are still many good, honest electricians around...

With warm regards

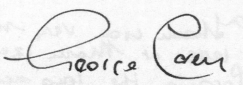

George Carey

MORELLO'S MENAGERIES

Park View Road
Ealing
London W5
25 March 2006

Sir Richard Branston
Chief Executive
Virgin Group Limited
Campden Hill Road
London W8 7AR

Dear Sir Branston

May I congratulate you on the Virgin empire of companies – Mrs Morello and I reckon your products are exellent in every department. The Mrs, whose in charge of spending the money, says we particularly like the trains and planes and also the wedding dresses (although I anticiprate there are none in her particular size at this junction in time as they don't exist). She likes to flick through the mags and squeeze into the matrimonial equipment as a possible hint whenever I'm in the doge's house with respect to any misdemeanour regarding the Mrs eg if I haven't fed the emus for a couple of days because I forgot etc.

However there is a small stone in the Mrs' shoe with regard to the empire which she wishes to shake out   Last Saturday we picked up a couple of tins of the new **Branston Baked Beans** from Tresco's. We and the kids had one for tea with some codpieces.

Unfortunately the Mrs states that we found the taste pleasant though somewhat unusual. Also that the beans themselves were rather chewy though we noted that Desmond the emu quite enjoyed them. And Angus the hairy bullock

 I appreciate living on a boat you may not be that near the shops but there used to be beans you could buy and eat without unusual consequences overnight. Anyway the wife advises that the whole thing can be overlooked if you could arrange for her to have a State visit to your holiday home which I understand is an island (Necher Isle) for a couple of weeks with some expenditures thrown in.

I understand the Mrs wishes to travel alone, with me staying at home with the mammals. So I would enter a small plea for her to have a third week too. (Maybe I could complain a bit about something else we ate and say it tasted like slugdeath or something?) Also Titan the toy poodle ate some turkeyburgers and was sick everywhere.
Hoping to hear soon.

Yours sincerely

RM Morello (Mr)

Management

Our ref: dg/060406/ls

06 April 2006

Mrs Morello
Park View Road
Ealing
London
W5

Dear Mrs Morello

Many thanks for your letter addressed to Richard Branson.

Because Richard is currently travelling for so much of his time, I'm afraid he is unable to do justice to your request.

I'm so sorry.

Kind regards

Lynne Saville
Virgin Management Ltd

Virgin Management Ltd
The home of Virgin

120 Campden Hill Road, London, W8 7AR   Telephone: +44 (0)20 7313 2000 Facsimile: +44 (0)20 7727 8200
Registered in England & Wales No. 1568894

virgin.com

MORELLO'S MENAGERIES

Park View Road
Ealing   London W5
27 March 2006

The Top Mediator
United Mediators (Mediation Service)
Sandford Gate
Sandy Lane West
Oxford OX1 6LB

Dear Sir or Madam

I understand you are an outfit that steps in fast to stop people suing each other at the law courts and then gets them to have a chat to sort matters out. I do hope you can help.

Whereas normally the wife reads nothing but gift catalogues and crossword solvers, recently she's been spending ages studying a fat little book containing all the rules and regs for the local bowls club.

Now there's been an unpleasant coup down at the club – involving the wife (Rosetta) and two of her competitors for the Club Secretary's job, which fell vacant after all that business with Wally Hibbert and the Japanese waitress when he visited the Blue Parrot night club. Mrs M has engineered a situation where she's seized power at the bowls club by outwitting Dot Partridge and Bunty Bagshawe, two longserving committee members who were standing for election as Club Secretary.

First, the Mrs told me she'd had a *"special word"* with Dot last Saturday morning when they were both under the hairdryers at Irene's Hair Salon for curlers and a full set, in preparation for the elections at the clubhouse that evening. Within about 5 minutes of the chat Dot had sped from the salon and immediately written to all the committee members withdrawing from the contest and stating what an excellent candidate the Mrs was. She also dropped round an envelope at our house containing £25 for the wife towards the new piranha tank we're installing in the lounge.

Secondly, it was claimed that the wife had threatened Bunty with Desmond, our emu, in the ladies' locker room last Tuesday. Then, on the Saturday afternoon, Desmond was seen in the club car park beside Ted Figgis's Ford Anglia kicking out violently at Bunty. Bunty copped one in the solar plexus and was urgently removed to St Chad's for a full check up. So she missed the elections that evening.

Now the Mrs has been elected unopposed. She's since claimed the rules allow her as Secretary to treat all the club greens as *"grazing and leisure space"* for our animals, under *"ancient rights"*. As we run a little menagerie for kiddies and OAPs including goats, ostriches, a couple of camels and a quite dangerous venomous Italian ocelot this line of thought could be deemed socially irresponsible.
Anyway now everyone's talking about suing each other. Could you come up with an early crompromise eg where the animals only use say Greens 1 and 2 on Tuesday mornings? Also, would you wish to inspect Desmond, and can you take evidence from Bunty in hospital?

Hoping to hear soon. Don't tell the wife I wrote in.
Yours sincerely

RM Morello (Mr)

18 April 2006

Mr R.M Morello
Park View Road
Ealing
London W5

Your Ref: mediation service
Our Ref: Legal/MP
Please quote this reference in all correspondence

Dear Mr Morello

Ealing Bowls Club

Please excuse the delay in responding to you. I am 'The Top Mediator' here (in terms of settlement rates, length of service, seniority and qualification) and it sometimes takes time for my many underlings to sort *bona fide* letters from the idiocy I frequently receive.

My usual role is to provide a mediation service for those involved in DRS service. However, as a fellow emu owner and ocelot wrangler, I empathise with your wife's plight. Where is one to find grazing, except that enshrined in the ancient rights of this fair land? Bowls clubs, like golf courses, are clearly fair game for grazing our game (if you'll pardon my little pun).

As a veteran pedant, I could not help noticing that some of your animals are very old: 'OAPs including goats, ostriches, a couple of camels...' I do hope your elderly animals die soon, as this will clearly help your difficult situation and provide meat for the table.

As a prelude to successful mediation, I have taken the liberty of contacting Wally, Dot, Bunty, Irene's Salon and the Blue Parrot Bar. I intend to use what community mediators call 'Gestalt Mediation'. At this early stage I would suggest a preliminary meeting at the Blue Parrot to discuss the rules by which we will meet at Irene's Salon to discuss the rules of the mediation to be held at the Bowls Club.

I understand that this might seem like a very blunt way of approaching your dispute, but I must recommend this direct approach to your problem.

Yours sincerely

Mike Penman
The Top Mediator

END OF CORRESPONDENCE

MORELLO'S MENAGERIES

Park View Road
Ealing
London W5

2 April 2006

The Manager
Seymour Leisure Centre
Seymour Place
London W1

Dear Sir

Hello! I'm Mr Morello and an Italian gent. All our family loves your pool and the staff and we come along for a swim and shower etc and use the hairdryers quite a lot whenever we can leave the animals to look after themselves without fighting etc.

Unfortunately we've got a problem at the moment what with the water supply to the fishtanks in the back garden. **So our youngest, Rizzo (7), whose always swimming asks is it OK if we roll up one day with our baby tiger shark for a bit of a swim and a work out? He's called Eamonn and is a really nice, friendly little fellow.** (He's named after a chum of ours, Eamonn Whelan, who runs a horsefair over near Drayton somewhere who sold us our tiny thoroughbred Shetland pony, Thunderbolt, who looks a bit rough but has proved a great hit with the kids and OAPs down the menagerie).

Don't worry about Eamonn the sharklet - he'll be wearing goggles to keep out the chlorine. Anyway, he'd probably only nip anyone if they seem nervous. <u>Or if they move around too much.</u> So maybe we could slip him in the deep end when there's only a few older bathers in as they don't move so much.

Hoping to hear soon otherwise we'll bring Eamonn along some time before Easter if that's ok unless you say it isn't etc.

If you do lane swimming, he should definitely be in the **fast** lane as he can shift a bit.

Anyway the wife won't be coming as she's a bit heavy on the displacement side to do with being somewhat bulky etc which could flood the cubicals.

All the best

Yours sincerely

RM Morello

RM Morello (Mr)

PS: Any chance you could have a couple of buckets of sardines standing by, poolside, in case Eamonn gets a bit peckish after the exercise? Or cod.

R M Morella
Morello's Menageries
Park View Road
Ealing
London
W5

6th April 2006

Dear Mr. Morello,

Thank you very much for your letter dated 2nd April 2006.

At Seymour Leisure Centre we are always looking for ways to improve the service we provide to our customers, and we are delighted that you are enjoying the use of the pool, showers, and hair dryers.

Where we can, we try to accommodate all requests made by our members and customers, but unfortunately we are unable to accommodate your son, Rizzo's, request to bring your beloved baby tiger shark, Eamonn. Maybe sometime in the future we will be able to accommodate you by being able to build a fish tank with adequate non chlorine water supply so that Eamonn will not have to wear goggles.

If we are able to provide the fish tank in the future maybe you will be kind enough to recommend someone who can supply us with sardines or cod.

Once again thank you for your letter, and we hope to see you and your family (without the animals) in the Centre soon.

Yours sincerely,

Abbey Beyene
Administration Manager

City of Westminster
Leisure for Life

Registered Office: Cannons House, 40-44 Coombe Road, New Malden, Surrey KT3 4QF
Registered in England No. 2849324   VAT No. 437 1039 67

Seymour Leisure Centre

MORELLO'S MENAGERIES

Park View Road
Ealing
London W5

18 April 2006

Professor Sir Stanley Wells
Chairman
The Shakespeare Birthplace Trust
Stratford on Avon
Warwickshire

Dear Prof Sir Stanley

Hello! I would like to introduce myself as Mr Morello. I am writing to you as an eminent scholar and researcher into the question of the Bard of England, sweet Swan of Avon etc.

Whenever a new influx of creatures etc arrives at our menageries here we have a Grand Opening Ceremony involving as often as not a celebrity appearance to induct the beasts and make them homely and at ease surrounded by our kids and various other animales.

By the by the Mrs and me have just received delivery of a pile of new goats. They're quite a ragbag of critters involving Boers, pygmies, northern tufted straightbacks and a couple of quite rare Devon bluenecks.

But there's one particular beast that is unquestionately aside and apart from the rest. He's a superb specimen – tall, dignified, with a lovely white silky coat and long snowy beard. He stands aloof and magnificent in the stinging nettles in the corner of the garden, keeping his own counsel, silently surveying the daily scene unfolding about him with pale blue knowing eyes. Mrs Morello (Rosetta) and myself have had some heated debate about a suitable name for this paradigm. Despite disagreements (fur flying etc) we 've finally agreed the name should be........**Shakespeare.**

We're planning the animals' induction for **Sunday 21 May**. We realise it would be a long way to come and that you must be very busy, but the wife says we would be delighted if you would graciously consent to pop your head in to the goat's Opening.

We could of course collect you off the train at say Ealing Broadway or West Acton or even Hanger Lane and top you up with some sandwiches and a wagon wheel on the way home, and an apple.

Hoping to hear soon. Thanks for your help.

Yours sincerely

RM Morello (Mr)

PS: The wife enquires whether you prefer sardine or fishpaste?

Dear Mr Morello,

Sorry to be slow in replying – I've been in Romania.

Thanks very much for your entertaining invitation. I'm sure it would be great fun to meet you, your wife, and the new Shakespeare, but as the date you suggest is my birthday it wouldn't go down all that well at home! I hope you have a very successful day.

Best wishes

Stanley Wells

THE ST FINBARR'S RAMBLERS ASSOCIATION

Park View Road
Ealing
London W5

6 May 2006

Sir Cliff Richard
Cliff Richard Organisation
PO Box 46c
Esher
Surrey KT10 0RB

Dear Sir Cliff

Please may I introduce myself. I am Mrs Morello and the Secretary to the St Finbarr's Ramblers Association (founded 1926). We are a group of like-minded folk of all sorts and ages who wander around the countryside singing and chanting happy songs about nature and birds etc, and picking a few flowers as we go, and herbs.

We love all of God's creation including fauna as well as flora, so this year we're introducing a few emus into the walks, and a couple of llamas or possibly a meerkat which one of our members recently inherited. **The emus will be led on a bit of string as they get nervous walking round lots of corners. So we're going to try to walk as far as possible in a straight line.**

We've got a packed programme this season, and you may be excited to know we'll be in your area **during a Sunday afternoon in May or early June.** As we're starting out from the local railway station and going north north west, our Chairman has calculated that on the line to be taken the whole group expects to bisect your back garden, probably at around 3.15 to 3.45pm. We hope that's ok but if not hoping to hear soon and we can try to alter the route a bit, and experiment with little hoods for the emus. Several of our members, who are sun worshippers, like to walk stark naked (except for sandals and rucksacks), but can cover up if passers-by express a strong personal preference. No dogs allowed.

If you feel you would be interested in joining us on a ramble, or linking up with us as we trudge through your garden please do. Please bring some stout footwear for comfort, and waterproofs. A modest contribution is requested. It would be particularly joyful if you could bring a guitar and lead us in some of our songs as we all tramp along, rather like at Wimbledon when it's raining, during the interludes before Tim Henman gets beaten.

We have some nice packed lunch ideas, and also some useful tips for getting your first Blue Peter badge. Look forward to hearing soon. All the best.

Yours sincerely

Rosetta Morello (Mrs)

Hon Chairman: The Rt Rev Maurice Flambard DD MA
Hon Treasurer: Betty Trubshaw (Mrs)

SIR CLIFF RICHARD

GS/SW

17 May 2006

Mrs Rosetta Morello
Park View Road
Ealing
London W5

Dear Mrs Morello

Thank you for your letter of 6 May to Sir Cliff Richard.

While Sir Cliff would be delighted to have his privacy invaded by a group of warbling nudists, he regrets that, due to the undesirable side-effects of his acute llama allergy, he is unable to offer hospitality to your group on any May or June afternoon.'

Yours sincerely

Cliff Richard Organisation

Park View Road
Ealing
London W5
6 May 2006

Ms Polly Toynbee
The Guardian Newspaper
119 Farringdon Road
London EC1R 3QR

Dear Ms Toynbee

I believe you are an eminent journalist and leading proponent of atheism.

Please may I introduce myself. I am RM Morello and an Italian gent. I was once an atheist who didn't believe in God or any of His Works. However I became so disgusted about the permissive society and it's pervasive effect with respect to everything (TVs, microwaves, eclectic blankets etc) that I got rid of the lot and got involved in the druidical movement.

I gradually began to realise from first principles that there must be something in the "Godworshippers" as I had termed them. After all if no God exists around the place, how come we've got all these churches and bishops, and days off like Easter Sunday, Xmas Day and the rest (which apart from anything are a blessed relief from more shopping days etc). Then when I realised the strange things the druids get up to "Under the Oaks" as they put it, I reported them to the RSPCA and became a C of E. Anyway we met quite a nice bloke on holiday in Tenerife who turned out to be a bishop with a time share.

The final camel over the straw's back was a horrendous evening in Weymouth where me and the Mrs (Rosetta) were having a long weekend away from the kids. We were strolling along the foreshore on the promenade when we came upon a massive din outside the so called Ethical Hall. **What was going on was an almighty punch up between the atheists and the agnostics. This had spilled out onto the street, with bottles, fists and certain words flying around, a bit like the rods and mockers way back in the 1920s or whatever.** The whole scene was a disgrace, and in no way fitting for a responsible group of disbelievers (or uncertains). That said, the atheists acquitted themselves well and definitely got the better of their doubting opponents, who seemed somewhat non-committal and so left themselves vulnerable to sudden jabs and blows.

The modern church is by no means perfect in all its parts and as I regard myself as a bit of a freethinker, I would quite like to re-become an atheist whilst having half a foot in the Anglican world.

May I ask if there are any books you could recommend me and the Mrs to read in order to get attuned to secularism, before we commit ourselves to a Godless world? We may need to do this gradually to avoid upset on the Parish Committee where Mrs Morello traditionally helps out with the Christmas bric a brac.

Many thanks, God bless

Yours sincerely

RM Morello (Mr)

15th May 2006

Dear Mr. Morello.

Many thanks.   I would suggest a book by Professor
Richard Dawkins.   Extraordinary story from
Weymouth!

Yours sincerely,

Polly Toynbee

119 Farringdon Road
London EC1R 3ER

ACKNOWLEDGEMENTS

This project began over ten years ago with the issue of a few random letters, sent forth for the amusement of my nephews and nieces. Some delightful and surprising replies were received. Interest grew and events gathered pace. A more concentrated venture took shape. The man from Basildon Bond was summoned and Mrs Morello's escritoire was placed on full alert.

I must thank all those who have encouraged me during the process of helping the Morellos in the writing of their letters and all those others who, having received such a communication, have troubled themselves to reply.

Acknowledgments of support and help, being of necessity selective, are invidious. But from the former category I wish especially to mention the following: Robin and Tessa Ingram, Roger Murphy, Ian McKendry, Brian Cronin, Miguel and Vicky Fiallos, Joan Hammett, Robin Wells, Philip Groves, Fiona Rubens, Lynette d'Souza, Graham Rolt, Chloe Williams, David Emmett, Julie and Alice Young, Dennis Pinkstone, Sarah Macken, Elizabeth Haylett, Carla Mandis, Frank Wessely and Dr Raymond Lobo. Friendship is a high estate but surely recognises no obligation to suffer an author's desire to be heard barking like a variety of dogs in alternate moods, less still to be subjected to his notion of the noise emanating from a cockatoo when it espies a ghost in the Morellos' back garden. Yet these privations and others of similar character have been borne with fortitude by many of the foregoing in the course of this book's production.

As to the latter category, I wish to renew my thanks to all

the statesmen, archbishops, atheists, aristocrats, taxidermists, celebrity superstars, librarians, millionaires, toilet paper manufacturers, mediators, goat club proprietors, plastic surgeons, bardologists, bankers and nudists (and many others) without whose generous epistolary intervention this book would have amounted to no more than a worthless exercise in writing to oneself.

But I am bound also to acknowledge my debt to those cousins of the above who provided the early and much of the sustaining inspiration for setting out in print the Morellos' way of life: all the howling, screeching, panting, roaring, rustling, scratching, snuffling, hopping, flailing, bleating and chirping creatures of the animal kingdom. They hold a special place in the hearts of the Morellos, and in the author's too.

From this personal chaos emerges the happy and perplexing world of the Morello family which is, and will remain always, one of profound discombobulation.

I must record my appreciation to my friends at Monster Publications for their refulgent wisdom and their support.

Finally my grateful and sincere thanks to all those copyright holders for permission to reproduce their correspondence.

July 2006